3 1299 00424 4241

D1374324

B                    /alt.

          Law v.  life.


     $17.95

| DATE | | | |
|---|---|---|---|
|  |  |  |  |
|  |  |  |  |
|  |  |  |  |
|  |  |  |  |
|  |  |  |  |
|  |  |  |  |
|  |  |  |  |
|  |  |  |  |
|  |  |  |  |
|  |  |  |  |
|  |  |  |  |
|  |  |  |  |
|  |  |  |  |

East Meadow Public Library
Front St. & East Meadow Avenue
East Meadow, L.I., N.Y. 11554

BAKER & TAYLOR

# LAW V. LIFE

# LAW v. LIFE

*What Lawyers Are
Afraid to Say about
The Legal Profession*

## WALT BACHMAN

*Four Directions Press*
*Rhinebeck New York*

LAW V. LIFE: *What Lawyers are Afraid to Say about The Legal Profession*
Copyright © 1995 by Walt Bachman. All rights reserved. Printed in the United
States of America. No part of this book may be used or reproduced in any
manner whatsoever without written permission of the publisher except in the
case of brief quotations embodied in critical articles and reviews. For information address Four Directions Press, P.O. Box 417, Rhinebeck, New York 12572,
800-556-6200.

FIRST EDITION


International Standard Book Number: 0-9627659-8-8
Library of Congress Catalog Card Number: 95-60315


Book design by Sean McCarthy & Sally Keil

# CONTENTS

∽

# LAW V. LIFE

# *A Life in the Law: Image and Reality*

Sexual abuse by the clergy, insider stock trading, domestic violence, corporal punishment in the schools, abortion (or fetus) rights, the clash between protecting spotted owls and the right to clear-cut Pacific old growth forests—name any controversy that enthralls, enrages or engages the American public, and lawyers are at its forefront. Lawyers are at the cutting edge of every issue, public or private, that defines or divides our country. Delicate and explosive matters that in past generations were dealt with by religious leaders, politicians, business executives, parents, and teachers—or that weren't dealt with at all—are thrust these days into the hands and briefcases of lawyers. Lawyers are everywhere today.

Clients, who beget lawyers, are everywhere as well, both as plaintiffs and defendants. No one is exempt from the pervasive impact of the legalizing of American culture. The powerful, be they corporate or individual, are targets for legal comeuppances as never before. We lionize the lawyers whose lawsuits bring to their knees some of the world's largest corporations. School administrators who once feared only a wrathful PTA or school board now are held accountable in court, and their discretion is circumscribed by ever more laws and rules. We appoint special prosecutors and give them a roving, nebulous mandate to bring down our presidents. Painful personal travails once handled with hushed private discretion, such as incest, marital abuse, punishment of children, or death with dignity, have all entered the realm of legal regulation, producing lurid lawsuits that are often accompanied by blaring headlines. Whether you agree or disagree with its reach into every tiny fissure in American society, the law dominates our personal and collective decision-making to an unprecedented extent.

Read John Grisham's or Scott Turow's novels, or see *The Client*, *Philadelphia*, *The Pelican Brief* or any other contemporary movie dealing with the law, and you will encounter countless images of lawyers leading exciting lives, filled with intellectual and idealistic crusades. Even sole practitioners operating out of faded offices and tattered briefcases are endowed with the power to slay the modern equivalents of fairy tale ogres and Goliaths. Lawyers are agents for sports heroes, drive Maseratis, and represent movie stars in divorces. Deciding the fascinating disputes that flow through our courts are judges, all of whom are lawyers.

Then there is the money. Tens of thousands of lawyers make more than a quarter of a million dollars a year, more than eight times the average income for a family of four. A typical corporate lawyer in a big law firm is paid more than all but a few of the top executives in the largest companies he or she advises—and much more than even the highest executives of his or her small or mid-sized clients.

Is it any wonder that law schools are inundated with applications and can choose to admit only the brightest of those desiring to embark on legal careers? Or that successful law school applicants willingly shoulder student loan baggage averaging $50,000 or more for the opportunity of taking the bar examination? Or that law firms with a single opening for a new lawyer often receive more than 200 resumés?

The last 25 years have encompassed a complete transformation not only in the legal profession, but in the very role played by law—and lawyers—in America. This period has brought more legal practitioners, more laws, more lawsuits and many more problems that are framed in legalistic terms.

My own years in the law have spanned this same quarter-century. Those years began in England in 1966 with a tutorial studying torts at Oxford University and culminated in my handling multimillion dollar cases as a litigation partner in a major law firm. More than most lawyers in an age of legal specialization, I have found myself in a wide variety of practices—small firm and large, public and private, representing both poor clients and corporate giants. While I never strayed far from my first love, trial practice, my cases ranged from divorces to dog bites, from murders to massive antitrust cases, from lawyer disbarment prosecution to personal injury claims.

I graduated from Stanford Law School in 1970, in the heyday of law firm expansion, before the revolutionary impacts of lawyer advertising, before the transformation of law from a classic profession to a market-oriented business, and before the legal job market became glutted. It was a time when neither clients nor lawyers jumped freely from one law firm to another, when it was unethical to list your firm's name in bold-face type in the phone book (Yellow Pages and newspaper advertising was unthinkable), and when the graduates of good law schools had virtually unlimited opportunities. I was offered a job at every one of the ten law firms with which I interviewed, including the largest firms in San Francisco and Wall Street, as well as in my home state of Minnesota. In those days of explosive law firm growth, we law school seniors interviewed firms as much as we were ourselves interviewed, and we debated among the employment alternatives, picking and choosing with relative ease. Virtually all of my classmates also got good jobs before graduation. Today we would all be facing a very different world, for the majority of law students are not employed at the time they get their JDs.

Largely due to a desire to return to my roots and to raise a family in the Midwest, I joined a prominent law firm in Minnesota. Almost immediately, I became frustrated in the role of a beginning associate. On my third successive weekend researching the esoteric points of the Internal Revenue Code's application to a multi-national corporation, staring at the law firm library wall, I impulsively decided that hanging out my shingle for divorce clients on Lake Street, a somewhat tawdry Minneapolis thoroughfare bordered by used car lots and massage parlors, would be better than this. I quit on the spot, without the slightest idea what I would be able to line up for myself. I yearned to be a trial lawyer, not a back-room associate assisting senior lawyers in preparing documents.

Within a month, l linked up with two other lawyers, a young partner in the firm I was in and a corporate lawyer, and we each left our jobs to co-found a new firm in the fast-growing suburb of Bloomington, Minnesota. Less than a year out of law school, I found myself a name partner and the only trial lawyer in a small firm. Over the $2.99 steak special at a restaurant located across the freeway from our sterile office park, my new partners and I joked about having enough work to keep us busy for about a month and signed a five-year lease. After showing the bank a financial statement that revealed a negative net worth due to law school loans, I was able to borrow enough to pay my share of the rent, secretaries, and office expenses for a six-month start-up period.

In those early days, we didn't even wait for a potential client to finish a sentence starting with "Do you handle my type of case, which is...?" before we said "yes." We did *everything*, at least until we had enough work to pay the bills. We accommodated clients on fees just to keep busy. On one occasion, we all drove out to a client's Lake Minnetonka bait shop and loaded up on minnow buckets and monofilament fishing line as in-kind payment of an overdue billing. I once accepted a mounted flying squirrel as payment from an amateur taxidermist.

Like many earnest young lawyers at the time, I also represented *pro bono* clients. One was a memorable 17-year-old escapee from juvenile jail, who was told at a drop-in center for teens that I handled juvenile cases without charge and who showed up with no forewarning in our reception room.

He wanted to turn himself in, he said, and to prove that he was railroaded into a wrongful conviction. Amazingly, his story was both compelling and true, and he was sprung by a judge on the grounds that his "confession" was coerced. The "voluntary incriminating statements" taken by the police on a drug charge had actually been made while the boy's father was beating him up in a cell, and he also had been denied legal counsel at his trial.

Time and again, I found myself poring over handbooks and legal journals far into the night to learn how to approach a case that was scheduled in court the next morning. It was at that stage that my prematurely graying hair yielded its greatest benefits, for seldom did clients, judges, or adversaries suspect my total inexperience with evictions, arraignments, or all the other legal proceedings new to me. Not uncommonly, a day's work included a deposition in a whiplash case, a court appearance on a child support motion in divorce court, and a conference with a landlord client about unpaid rent claims. I shudder now to think of the breadth of cases I handled with so little experience, though somehow most of them ended with reasonably good results.

The upward slope of my learning curve in those initial years was steep. The heady satisfaction of mastering a new skill came at the cost of awakening on countless occasions at 3:00 a.m. with the panicky thought that I had overlooked a legal issue or fact necessary to my practice schedule for the upcoming day. By the end of my five years in that small-firm practice, I felt comfortable as a trial lawyer, confident that I could carry almost any case from initial client interview to jury trial to appeal, if necessary. Moreover, our little firm had prospered, growing from three to ten lawyers. The big firm I left had also flourished, but I never regretted leaving its library for good that day.

At that juncture, at the ripe age of 31, I was ready again for a change. While the small firm trial practice had satisfied my desire for first-chair trial experience, it left deeper altruistic leanings unfulfilled. I had come of age in the era symbolized by the creation of the Peace Corps. The prospect of continuing to build a thriving suburban law practice for another thirty years felt incomplete. Indeed, doing anything for another thirty years seemed unthinkable.

Early in 1976, I responded to a mailing sent to all Minnesota lawyers by a Minnesota Supreme Court search committee seeking a new director of the office responsible for investigating and prosecuting lawyers' ethical violations. This was the post-Watergate period, when the entire country watched in fascination as a parade of defendants, most of them lawyers, went from high office to prison. Local stories of miscreant lawyers had been woven by the press into the Watergate theme of a profession rocked by scandal and misconduct, a profession without ethical underpinnings, a theme that still thrives. In this context, the committee was looking for a younger lawyer who could take a more visible and vigorous approach to the enforcement of Minnesota's legal ethics rules than had been taken in the past. The Court appointed me to the position. When I took office, both the search committee and members of the Court made clear their desire for heightened scrutiny of lawyers' practices in the state. I soon discovered that the confidential client complaint files held a backlog of serious lawyer misconduct cases, some of which had been languishing without resolution for several years.

The combination of a court and profession receptive to more stringent ethical regulation with a stockpile of unprosecuted cases led to a veritable deluge of highly publicized disbarment and other discipline trials. During my three years in that office, I believe more Minnesota lawyers were disbarred than in the preceding twenty. Because I held the prosecutorial reins as the profession's hired enforcer of ethical standards, I was called "law cop," "ethics czar," "Jaws," and many less flattering names by my fellow lawyers, although the vast majority of them then, as now, applauded strict enforcement of the rules of legal ethics. Since lawyers facing possible disbarment tend to hire the very best trial lawyers to defend themselves, I was privileged in my early 30's to try cases opposite some of the finest lawyers from criminal defense, personal injury, and business litigation practices, an opportunity not presented in other fields of law practice.

In 1979, a new criminal prosecutor was elected in Hennepin County (Minneapolis), and he asked me to become his Chief Deputy. For the next four years, almost every day brought delicate public policy conundrums that as a private lawyer I would never have had to contend with. When should a "sting" operation be used to combat crimes, and which ones? Should a welfare mother with three kids be sent to jail for welfare fraud? When should a wiretap be authorized? This job routinely required me to differentiate between the effective use of government power and the abusive or misdirected use of that power, issues more moral and ethical than legal.

But my main responsibility was helping to supervise an office of 75 civil service, unionized attorneys, most of whom had been appointed to their positions by the man whom their new boss had defeated. It proved to be my most frustrating legal job. Whenever a vacancy occurred, I spent endless tedious hours maneuvering through the civil service system to attempt to hire the best qualified attorney as a replacement. Like a managing partner of a private firm, I found my days filled less with the law than with personnel, policy, and administrative crises. My head told me I was having a bigger impact on criminal law enforcement than any of the prosecutors I supervised, but my heart told me they were doing the real work.

I found myself envying the day-in-court work fare of most of the lawyers in the trenches, discovering in the process that even momentous policy issues were, for me, not a sufficient substitute for the hands-on case work of a trial lawyer. I jumped at the chance to present the state's murder cases to the grand jury, even though it took only ten per cent or so of my time. I longed to be on the front lines rather than behind a desk supervising. When faced with a choice of reading a case file or attending a policy-setting committee meeting, I always wanted to opt for the former, though the job required much more of the latter. It was a lesson well worth learning, for I thereafter resisted any urge to stray far from a trial practice.

I returned to private practice in 1983, coming full circle back to a large law firm, partly to assure my three children a college education. My work focused on one or two huge cases at a time, virtually all of them multimillion dollar business disputes ranging from commercial trade secret cases to business fraud to antitrust. My income more than quadrupled from the highest salary I'd received as a public lawyer.

My time was billed at $200 per hour, about as much as any Minneapolis lawyer charged.

All in all, I have experienced some of the best of American careers in law. As a consequence, I'm in a better position than most to describe the many satisfactions a law practice can offer from the standpoint of prestige, respect, income, and intellectual challenge. On balance, I benefited greatly from a profession that, at its best, is a high calling.

And yet I find myself dwelling on the reaction I received from colleagues when I announced my resignation as a firm partner recently in order to write, teach, and pursue a more service oriented path. Time and again, lawyers at the pinnacle of their careers telephoned me or came into my office (usually closing the door discreetly behind them so as not to be overheard) to reveal their secret aspirations for escaping from their lives in the law. The recurrent themes of these emotion-laden conversations were disillusionment, lack of satisfaction, and a sense of hand-wringing dismay over the direction the legal profession had taken. Lawyers making up to a third of a million dollars a year expressed their vision of chucking it all to run a bait shop in northern Minnesota, teach inner-city kids, or manage a symphony orchestra. Some told me they were actively squirreling away money to finance their fantasies. Most were just dreaming aloud, considering themselves pinioned for life to their legal careers by the golden handcuffs of a partner's income.

How can so many who occupy a position of privilege in a profession so favored be so unhappy with their lives? What has happened to those of us who left law school in the '60's and '70's with such grand visions of altruism and challenge? Why do legions of lawyers whose main goals were to serve and help now wish only to get out? What lessons have we learned in the years since law school? What can we say to those now considering or starting a legal career?

A gaping chasm exists between the image and the reality of lawyering in America. Weighing my many positive experiences as a lawyer against its more troubling aspects, I keep coming back to the truths about lawyers most likely to be overlooked or denied, the unseen disquieting parts of lawyers' lives, those shaded crannies not viewed with any clarity until after many years in practice, if ever. For me, the lessons of the following chapters are true, whether or not they tell the whole story.

Even before I entered law school, I knew the potential benefits of becoming a lawyer—the challenge, the excitement, the power, the prestige, the idealism, the money. In large measure, I have found all of these and more as a law student and lawyer.

This book deals with other lessons, those I wish I'd learned in law school, but didn't.

∞

# CHAPTER ONE

# *The Monkey's Burden*

I n these days of rampant workaholism in the law, there
is a tendency to equate the inordinate stresses of legal
practice with the long hours worked. This equation is
partly correct, but the number of hours billed does not fully
account for the stressed-out condition of American lawyers.

My grandfather worked hours fully as long as those I have
spent in a law office, but the impact upon our lives of these
equal labors is anything but equivalent. Grandpa was in the
floral and gardening business, raising tomatoes for sale as
garden plants, carnations for use in floral arrangements, and
perennials for outdoor plantings. He worked on the growing side of things, leaving the business of planning,
accounting, and management concerns to others. Grandpa
was at work by 7:30, worked hard all day, and routinely put
in six-day weeks. He kept at it until he was 85, slowing a bit
only in the last few years. One of his favorite sayings was

"Hard work never killed anyone." In his line of work, I believe it was true.

As a teenager, I spent long hours working with Grandpa in the greenhouses transplanting coleus, snapdragon, and petunia seedlings in winter and in the perennial fields outdoors planting and tending phlox, delphinium, and other plants in summer. A full day potting geraniums or hoeing weeds among the perennials was physically draining. But the time spent in pleasing routine, guiding the growth of living things, in a super-oxygenated greenhouse or outdoors, led at the end of most days to a feeling of accomplishment and well-being. Moreover, the feeling of physical fatigue was not in conflict with focusing, at day's end, on friends, family, and other interests. The work was wearing, but not stressful. When I went from work in the greenhouse to doing homework for school, my mental alertness was actually enhanced. Problems with family or friends were easier, not more difficult, to contend with, and diversions such as a magazine or movie could command my full attention because there was no weight of daily concerns trailing me home from the workplace. Work complemented rather than clashed with my other activities and relationships. It's not surprising that Grandpa lived a long and healthy life.

Law practice, I found, is stressful in ways that Grandpa in his greenhouse never fathomed.

In my college social psychology class, we studied a series of scientific experiments with monkeys that were designed to test the physical impact caused by the stresses of responsibility. In one variation of the experiment, two monkeys were strapped side-by-side in chairs, with a control lever placed in front of each animal. For eight hours a day, electric shocks were delivered to both monkeys after the flashing of a warning light. If one of them pressed the lever in response to the warning light, both avoided the shock. There was a catch, however. Only one monkey's lever was actually connected to the electrical circuit; he was the responsible, or "executive," monkey, and he had the capacity to prevent the electricity from striking both monkeys. In this relatively straightforward variant of the experiment, neither monkey suffered any physical ill-effects, since the executive monkey was soon able to master the simple lever-pulling required.

The monkeys' experimental routine was then altered, and a second catch was added. Electric shocks could still be avoided by pressing the lever, but the shocks began to be administered at unpredictable times irrespective of the warning light. Try as he might, the executive monkey could only reduce the incidence of shocks, despite repeated lever-pulling. At this stage, nothing the executive monkey did could guarantee a totally pain-free existence for either monkey.

Aside from noting the perversity of the scientists who designed and carried out these experiments, I reacted strongly to the specter of these two restrained monkeys, and especially with pity for the "control" monkey with the useless lever, who was left utterly defenseless. Here he was, strapped into a chair under the watchful eyes of the observing scientists. No matter how many times he pulled the lever in front of him, he could have no influence over whether or when his life would be unpredictably interrupted by a nasty jolt. How miserable to sit there helpless, his comfort and peace of mind entirely dependent upon his neighbor's act to push the shock-avoidance lever. Feelings of powerlessness coupled with random electric shocks could put a real crimp in a chimp's life satisfaction level.

The responsible monkey, on the other hand, while he never got any more shocks than the dependent monkey, had greater control over the situation. Simply by pressing the lever with regularity, he could avert most shocks and get through an eight-hour stretch in the chair with only a few electrical irritants. Plus, he earned the bonus of protecting his companion at the same time.

The results of the experiments were a shock in themselves. All of the executive monkeys died from inflamed ulcers within weeks, while the powerless monkeys showed no signs of physical maladies. Since both monkeys received the same electrical shocks, neither the fear of harm nor the actual harm experienced could account for the death of the monkey burdened with control of the shock-avoidance lever. Apparently, the executive monkeys all died from the stress of professional responsibility.

The findings of the monkey experiments apply to any type of executive position in which responsibility is accompanied by an inability to control all of the important variables that can lead to disastrous results. Lawyers, business managers, and government administrators are all prime candidates for the stressed-out fate of the executive monkeys, whether they suffer from ulcers, heart attacks, or mental breakdowns.

From time to time as a practicing lawyer, especially when the strains of dealing with a difficult client increased the stress level to a temporary zenith, I have found my thoughts returning to the monkey experiments. Extrapolating to my own circumstances, I visualized hominoid variants of those experiments, mentally substituting a strapped-in lawyer for the executive monkey, sitting side-by-side with a client in lieu of the control monkey. In my daydream experiments, of course, the client and lawyer could speak to one another, thereby adding a degree of interchange absent in the simian versions. At the beginning, the sadistic scientists who controlled my imaginary experiments announced the penalties that would flow in the event of the lawyerly equivalent of failing to press the anti-shock lever (such as overlooking a relevant case, misgauging the judge's proclivities, or the like). In a stern voice, they intoned to the lawyer:

> "If you mess up, your client will...
> [Experiment One]...be imprisoned for twenty years.
> [Experiment Two]...be ruined financially.
> [Experiment Three]...have his or her reputation destroyed."

The experiment proceeded, with both scientist and client watchfully monitoring the lawyer's every move. One mistake by the lawyer led to immediate imposition of the pertinent penalty on the hapless strapped-in client, only to have another client seated in the chair for the next experimental round. Unlike the monkey experiments, *only* the client suffered direct pain from the lawyer's miscalculation or failure; the lawyer never went to jail or was ruined financially.

In refinements of my experimental daydreaming, I added the client's plaintive entreaties to the strapped-in lawyer:

> —"Don't screw up, lawyer. I'm counting on you. I don't think I could do twenty years of hard time," or

> —"My whole financial future's riding on you. You've just got to do the right thing," or

—"I've spent a lifetime building a stellar reputation, and you could ruin it with just one misstep."

To make the experiment yet more realistic, I visualized that the experimental client pressing the lawyer was often a flaming reprobate, one who likely deserved the consequences coming his or her way. No matter how detestable the client in my imaginary experiments, a dulcet-voiced, white-smocked scientist dispassionately admonished the lawyer over the experimental intercom system: "You are a professional. You must fulfill your duty to protect your client."

After reading this far, you might well be thinking that a mind this perverse deserves to be strapped into some kind of chair. But bear with me.

The monkey experiments, and my own variations of imagined lawyer/client take-offs, helped me understand why trial lawyers often suffer greater stress during a lawsuit than the client, whose future interest—or even liberty—hangs in the balance. With few exceptions, the shocks administered by the legal system can be handled in stride by the client. Even a prison sentence may be a more palatable outcome to the client than to the lawyer. The lawyer, who is professionally responsible for pulling countless levers in his or her attempt to solve the client's problems, often feels the heavier weight of stress than the client who suffers the actual loss. It seems to be part of the human, or primate, condition that the burden of responsibility for preventing something bad from happening, especially to others, is often worse than the painful occurrence itself.

Since a lawyer's primary role is to keep bad things from happening to others, the teachings of the monkey experiments are particularly apt, and provide the substance of one of several practical lessons that would have been useful to know when I graduated from law school to embark on a legal career.

> LESSON ONE: *Though the risks and consequences of a legal dispute are more dire for the client, it is often the lawyer who gets the ulcer.*

The risk inherent in all litigation is to lose, but the actual experience of defeat is often not as devastating as the contemplation of it. Trial lawyers have more opportunities than most to observe the resilient powers of even tragically defeated people.

Most lost lawsuits lead to setbacks in life, but almost never to the outright destruction of the loser. Furthermore, even the darkest legal cloud may have a silver lining. The grasping client whose cause is rejected by a rightfully judgmental jury may be slightly less greedy after the experience. The pigheaded, brook-no-opposition corporate executive may be chastened into a helpful newfound humility from a litigation defeat. Even the convicted felon can be renewed by the sense of atonement that flows from just punishment.

But these therapeutic side-effects of the legal process are felt almost entirely by the client. To the advocate, a loss is a loss. A bad result, even when the client deserves it, is hard to take.

Moreover, the vast bulk of a lawyer's time is spent in the stressful sphere of contemplating the *possibility* of loss rather than dealing with it in actuality. The seemingly interminable preparation for trial, replete with extended review of documents, depositions of witnesses, and prolix legal briefing of the facts and legal issues—all of which characterize the American legal system more than that of any other country and more than at any previous time in our history—occurs against the backdrop of the contemplation of a bad result. Even if every single lever is pulled at the right time and in the right way, there is no avoiding severe setbacks every bit as painful as electric shocks.

Ironically, the methods of modern litigation and the crush of cases clogging the courts make it a rarer and rarer event for an individual lawyer to suffer a clear-cut loss. Most cases grind to an inconclusive ending by settlement. Were we to endure more defeats, we might better understand the position of that powerless (and ulcer-free) experimental monkey, who simply concluded that an occasional electric shock is no big deal.

The monkey experiment variants are also instructive because they provide a mental picture of the most stressful aspect of lawyering—the individual client/attorney relationship. Lawyers whose trial practice career has straddled the public and private sectors, such as my own, often observe that a public practice is less stressful. The prosecution of even a high-profile criminal case can generate less stress on the lawyer than a small whiplash claim in private practice. The difference lies not in the difficulty of the lawsuit itself or in the societal significance or notoriety of the dispute, but rather in the burdensome focus of duty that derives from the responsibility for preventing harm to a specific person, and from seeking to achieve a result that is not only the best obtainable under law, but also satisfactory to that client. It is the individual client, figuratively strapped to the lawyer's side, who induces the ulcerous strains of private practice.

Public defenders, for example, are subject to earlier career burn-out than prosecutors because they, like private practitioners, represent individual, and in their case often wretched, clients. For the same reason, the struggle to save one prisoner on death row may be more stressful than the hardest-fought campaign to abolish capital punishment, though the lives saved (or lost) through the latter may be demonstrably greater. Similarly, many favor capital punishment, but few wish to serve as executioner.

The prosecutor, who champions the cause of the public interest—the amorphous many—usually finds it easier to leave the office behind at the end of the day. It is the specter of the fretful client, ever-present, ever-watchful, ever-concerned, calling the day after a court appearance to ask why a crucial point was not brought up, releasing a flood of personal worries, that is the lawyer's most stressful counterpart of the monkey's burden.

The total impact of stresses on lawyers is far greater than sum of the parts, more onerous than simply the mounting workload reflected in increased billable hours. Hard work alone cannot account for the well-documented ailments within the bar. The high incidence of depression that started in law school is also found later in a lawyer's life. Alcoholism afflicts a disproportionate number of lawyers, especially trial lawyers. Lawyers are prone to marital problems and divorce. Stress-related physical maladies—heart attacks, ulcers, strokes, high blood pressure—also hit lawyers hard, just as they did the responsible monkeys. From the standpoint of mental and physical health, the practice of law today must be viewed as a high-risk profession.

The private practice of law has a way of ferreting out and laying bare a lawyer's human shortcomings. The stresses imposed by the lawyer-client relationship can transform common personal peccadilloes into monsters, as I myself discovered early in my career, when a problem of ordinary procrastination became transformed into an obsessive nemesis.

About three years out of law school, as the trial lawyer in my small Minnesota firm, I agreed to take my first case of legal malpractice. It was against a local lawyer who appeared to have given incorrect tax advice to my client. After investigating the law and facts, I determined that a claim could be made, and I started the lawsuit. Once the case had gone down the pre-trial path for several months, I found myself putting this file at the end of my "to-do" list week after week. There were a number of legitimate reasons to pick up other files instead. It was not a large case, my client was rather unpleasant, the defense lawyer was of the intimidate-the-opposition school, and I was not very familiar with the law relating to malpractice.

One day, it dawned on me with some alarm that I had done nothing on this case for over six months. My client wasn't bugging me, and the irascible defense lawyer was perfectly content with my inaction. But from this point forward, this nagging file was never far from my thoughts, especially my "3:00 a.m. wake-up-in-a-cold-sweat" thoughts. As many times as I would resolve to move the case forward, I found myself inexplicably paralyzed to do anything about it.

For almost a year, this case became an episodic fixation. When I chanced upon magazine ads for mayonnaise, feelings of anxiety and dread swept over me simply because the product brand name was the same as that of my client. Just seeing his name was enough to bring on waves of guilt, shame, and self-anger.

I never did handle the case. Only after almost a year of inaction and worry did I finally summon the courage to confide my emotional paralysis to my partner. He immediately offered to take over the case, which he handled to a successful conclusion. Thus was lifted from me one of the greatest weights, self-inflicted though it was, of my life as a young lawyer. Had I been neglecting my own affairs, I could easily have shrugged off this single instance of procrastination. The sense of guilt flowing from mishandling another person's cause weighed infinitely more heavily.

Every busy lawyer has a cabinet full of active files, or, in the case of those whose office habits are as messy as mine, a desk or credenza strewn with files. Each file triggers a different personal reaction: some involve cases in which you feel supremely proficient and some raise questions you've never encountered before; some have been assigned to congenial and fair judges and some to judicial despots; some hold the papers of a client you have come to fear or detest; and some were a pleasant engagement until snarling Dan Doberman was substituted as counsel for the opposition. Thus, it is hardly surprising that lawyers do not approach all cases with equal attention or energy. Procrastination is a normal reaction to the things we dislike. For one reason or another, a lawyer tends to place certain files, again and again, at the bottom of the pile. This initially harmless form of delay can grow into one of the worst of a lawyer's recurring nightmares.

A lawyer's case files are like an endless series of probing tentacles, each feeling for one's peculiar shortcomings or weaknesses.

During the years I prosecuted legal ethics cases, I reviewed hundreds of files of ethics complaints by clients against lawyers, observing in the process the myriad ways in which troubles can arise in a law practice. Without question, I saw more lawyers thrown into emotional disarray from the seeds of simple procrastination blossoming into full-blown neuroses than from any other single source of difficulty. Sole practitioners are uniquely susceptible in this area, for they have no partners to whom they can turn for assistance as I did, to watch over them, or to whom their clients can complain. For just this reason, a far higher number of ethical complaints alleging neglect or delay are lodged by clients against sole practitioners than against lawyers who practice within a firm, and disproportionate numbers of sole practitioners are disbarred or disciplined.

The consequences of procrastination are more harsh in the legal profession than in other fields, partly because the nature of the work makes it harder to detect and partly because its impact can be severe on both lawyer and client. Under the best of circumstances, legal disputes are commonly protracted, sometimes over many years. It is much more difficult for the client to determine if his or her lawyer is procrastinating than, say, a plumber or an accountant. Virtually all clients will lose patience with the accountant who fails to meet the April 15 deadline or with the plumber who offers excuse after excuse for failing to come out to fix their leaky toilet. But a lawyer's clients have little notion of how long each stage of a lawsuit should take, and it may literally be years before they detect even the most flagrant procrastination by the lawyer. Which leads to the second, more serious, point: lawyer inaction can damage the client's claim or even deprive the client of a legal remedy by allowing the statute of limitations to run before a lawsuit is filed. Such serious instances of neglect can cause the lawyer more than the loss of a client. He or she may become a legal malpractice lawsuit defendant or may suffer the loss of professional license through discipline or disbarment.

It also became apparent to me during my ethics enforcement years that those who are tormented by what might be termed the Lawyers' Avoidance Syndrome are less likely to be deterred by threat of discipline or cured by psychological counseling, particularly in extreme cases, than almost any other type of conduct. Lawyers' Avoidance Syndrome—LAS—is a most resistant strain of affliction.

I recall one otherwise good lawyer who was placed on formal probation following a number of client complaints, the only principal condition being that he return telephone calls from clients inquiring about their cases within 48 hours. He was later disbarred when a single client produced records showing more than twenty successive unanswered long-distance calls over several months. Under order of the state Supreme Court to return telephone calls, he still lacked the ability to do so even upon pain of disbarment. I found that lawyers who had both chronic neglect and drinking problems could more readily stop drinking through treatment than cease harmful procrastination. While neurotic procrastinators are present in all fields of work, lawyers with LAS are in a position to do extreme damage to themselves and others. I would venture to guess that this problem is at the

core of many cases of what is diagnosed as d₍
anxiety.

From the episode I suffered myself and as an o₍
observer of the misery caused by this syndrome, I have noted
that LAS progresses in severity through four distinct stages
of behavior.

*LAS Stage One: Phobic Delay.* The LAS pattern always
begins with the equivalent of putting the client's file in the
back of the cabinet. The key to distinguishing LAS behavior from the prudent prioritizing of any busy lawyer's
workload is the linkage of the delay with something specific
the lawyer wishes to avoid, rather than with the overall crush
of time pressures. It is the difference between setting aside a
file because it requires several hours of uninterrupted time
to conduct legal research or review documents, for example,
and setting aside the file because you dislike the very idea of
talking with Dan Doberman again or because you regret
having accepted a case in an unfamiliar area. The former is
ordinary delay and the latter is Stage One LAS.

*LAS Stage Two: White Lies.* Sooner or later, the delaying
lawyer will be contacted by someone about the case, most
commonly the client, who will call to ask some version of
"How's my case coming along?" One of the telltale symptoms of LAS is the immediate knotting of the lawyer's
stomach that accompanies this call, an indicator that personal guilt, and not mere unpleasantness at facing a
disgruntled client, is rearing up. The response is often a white
lie citing something the lawyer needs to do but hasn't yet
done: "I've been working in the law library on a thorny
legal issue in your case" or "I've sent document demands to
the lawyer for the other side" or "It's in the mail." For many

lawyers, reaching this stage is sufficient to overcome the block that led to inaction, and they feel compelled to go to the law library, draft the document demand, or put "it" in the mail in order to make their statements "true."

*LAS Stage Three: Black Lies.* The foundation for this stage is normally the failure to follow through on previous white lie promises. Two characteristics separate this stage from Stage Two. First, the lawyer typically starts to place false blame on others. ("Doggone, that blasted lawyer hasn't gotten back to me yet on those document requests" or "I can't understand why they haven't responded to my letter" or "It must have been lost in the mails.") Second, by now there is likely to be written documentation of the lawyer's avoidance conduct, such as client letters innocently regurgitating earlier false assertions by the lawyer.

By the time Stage Three LAS has been reached, it is impossible to exaggerate the lawyer's daily emotional suffering. One otherwise completely decent and likable small-town lawyer, who was disbarred solely for chronic Stage Three-type conduct, told me: "You will never know what it's like to be me, to get up in the morning and be ashamed to look at myself in the mirror while shaving." For some, disbarment itself afforded real emotional relief from the hellish pain of responsibility for harmful, if unintended, conduct they were literally unable to control.

*LAS Stage Four: Invented Lawsuits.* As bizarre as it may seem, the crazy culmination of extreme LAS is the lawyer's creation of wholly fictitious lawsuits, stages of lawsuits, or even settlements. It is as though the false world the lawyer has created in Stages One through Three has become reality.

While highly unusual, there have been cases in which a divorce lawyer informed a client his or her divorce was final when, in actuality, the lawyer's LAS had led the case to languish in limbo, thereby creating unwitting bigamists. Other lawyers have paid a fictitious "settlement" out of their own funds (or funds diverted from partner accounts or other clients' trust accounts), rather than disclose chronic inaction. Such lawyers are not only disbarred, but often prosecuted as felons and bankrupted by subsequent lawsuits. While these cases form an infinitesimal fraction of the practicing bar, they depict the tragically self-destructive extremes of LAS, where in most cases there is no prospect of personal financial gain or underlying nefarious intent on the part of the lawyer.

It all started simply by putting one client's file on the bottom of the pile. And just as in the monkey experiments, it's the lawyer who gets the ulcer.

# CHAPTER TWO

## *Helping Till It Hurts*

For a former law partner of mine, frustration with her life as a trial lawyer was focused by the advent of parenthood. "Every day," she said over lunch, "I find myself doing things I teach my children not to do. At home, it's 'Children, don't fight.' 'Don't be mean.' 'Share your toys.' At the office, it's 'fight, fight, fight,' and grab what you can." Attending depositions with an especially obnoxious lawyer on the other side, she found herself suppressing the urge to send him to his room to cool down for awhile.

Like most law students, I chose law as a career because I viewed it as a helping profession. I don't deny that money, prestige, and power also entered the picture, but the vision of providing worthy service elevated law in my mind above the money-grubbing world of business. Law offered a higher calling. I envisioned myself as a White Knight, doing legal battle to right wrongs, protecting the peasants from the

marauding Black Knights, a kind of Floren
with a briefcase.

Even students who have no intention of d
lives to serving the downtrodden are lured by the concept
of lawyerly service. Doctors heal both rich and poor. Like-
wise, there is nothing dishonorable about providing legal
services to insurance companies or businesses or other clients who can well afford to pay legal fees. Even the rich are
entitled to justice under law. The image of the lawyer as a
helping professional offers a powerful motivation to the most
buttoned-down yuppie.

After my first five years of practice in a small firm, I was
still imbued with the notion of the helping lawyer. My divorce and personal injury clients, with some exceptions, were
grateful for my assistance. I could see my efforts had made a
real difference in many of their lives, guiding them through
difficult times of emotional or physical pain.

In this frame of mind, and on the heels of the lawyer-
embarrassing Watergate fiasco, I was proud to undertake
the job of enforcing the lawyers' code of ethics. Most non-
lawyers, I felt, were sorely misinformed about the great
lengths to which the legal profession goes to regulate the
conduct of its members. Speaking to civic groups, however,
I found I was likely to draw sniggers of disbelief at the very
term "legal ethics." As one Rotarian put it: "An ethical lawyer: Isn't that an oxymoron?"

I did my best to present an earnest defense of my profession. I pointed out that the rules of ethics governing
American lawyers are elaborate and detailed. In fact, I ex-
uded, the professional standards under which American
lawyers practice are far more explicit than the comparable

rules regulating any other trade or profession. The Rules of Professional Conduct, first adopted by the American Bar Association in 1970, form the basis of ethics codes enacted within each state. Far from an abbreviated set of platitudes, these rules more closely resemble a highly specific criminal code than the Ten Commandments.

Moreover, I emphasized that the primary thrust of these rules is to enshrine the duty of fidelity to the client. Conflict of interest rules, for example, attempt to assure unbridled loyalty to the client's cause by prohibiting all associations or influences that might undermine a lawyer's steadfastness. The rules also bind the lawyer, with very limited and well-defined exceptions, to maintain the secrecy of client confidences. A lawyer who handles client property or money is subject to the most rigorous fiduciary standards, right down to the type of bank accounts that must be maintained. Almost any impediment that would interfere with the lawyer's client-helping function is spelled out and controlled by rule, and the lawyer offending these standards faces vigorous investigation and discipline, including possible disbarment.

Most other professions, I told the Rotarians, rely largely upon unenforced ethical guidelines or have only vague and sketchy rules as the foundation for any type of ethical discipline of their ranks. During the 2400 years that separate the Hippocratic Oath from the current practice of medicine, doctors have progressed relatively little in the task of defining uniform enforceable standards for their colleagues. As a rule, the medical profession defers most difficult ethical quandaries to individual doctors to resolve on their own. While much is written about medical ethics, very little translates to, or is even directed at, a medical consensus as to conduct that is backed up by concrete rules. Significantly, there is no term for the removal of miscreant doctors that begins to approach the stigmatizing opprobrium of the disbarment of a lawyer.

Added to the detailed lawyers' ethical rules are interpretations by thousands of court decisions and by tens of thousands of published ethics opinions issued by various bar associations and committees. A review of these cases and opinions shows that the most grievous professional discipline is reserved for lawyers who stray from the duty to help clients. In the legal profession, taking client money or breaching a major duty owed to a client is the equivalent of an unpardonable sin, a lawyer's capital offense.

Moreover, the bureaucratic apparatus for enforcing the lawyers' rules of conduct is extensive. Virtually every state has at least one full-time "lawyer prosecutor," and the larger states all have large staffs whose sole job is to investigate alleged violations of the rules of legal ethics and to seek discipline of violators through disbarment or other proceedings. Considering both the scope of the rules and the means available for enforcing them, American lawyers are the most intensely regulated profession in the history of the world.

And yet, despite what I thought to be the ineluctable logic and wisdom of my speeches to civic groups, I discovered a persisting viewpoint that a reference to lawyers and ethics in the same breath is tantamount to misspeaking. Try as I might to dispel the idea, lawyers were seen as amoral, lacking any ethics in the ordinary sense. After my speeches, I would usually be complimented on my presentation—and then told stories about unethical lawyers who didn't care a whit about justice. At about this time, it dawned on me that non-lawyers see a side of the profession more clearly than the most ethical lawyers do—the hurting side.

Ironically, the aspect of lawyering most repugnant to non-lawyers flows from the very strength of the profession's ethical duty to help the client. The rules mince no words about the lawyer's obligation: "As advocate, a lawyer zealously asserts the client's position under the rules of the adversary system. [ABA Model Rules of Professional Conduct, Preamble]" The standard is to employ "zeal" on behalf of the client. This term, most commonly relegated to religious extremists and other fanatics in our society, is the cornerstone of American legal ethics.

Consider the role played by a zealous lawyer during trial. To advance the client's goals, it is not enough to tell the story through the mouths of friendly witnesses. Often, the outcome of the litigation depends more on tearing down the opposition's case through effective cross-examination.

By effective cross-examination, a lawyer can display a witness's innermost secrets or idiosyncratic foibles for all to see. An otherwise truthful witness may collapse upon being confronted with the fact that he was in the vicinity of the accident to visit a whorehouse. A witness with an uncontrollable, nervous laugh can be led through a number of somber questions by the cross-examiner who, when the irrepressible laugh escapes, thunders: "Do you consider this a laughing matter?" An unintelligent witness can sometimes be led to contradict his own testimony, or to cast doubt upon it through exposure of his mental shortcomings. The range of examples is as extensive and as limitless as the array of human behaviors and quirks. And behind it all, the cross-examining lawyer is motivated—indeed ethically driven—not by a sense of justice, not by a desire for truth, not by fairness or decency, but always by the interests of the client.

Flowing from the overriding imperative of zealous advocacy is the duty to attack and, if possible, destroy a harmful witness by any means permitted by law. A trial lawyer, as the executioner of this obligation, wields a fearsome power. A prideful witness can be embarrassed, a vacillating witness made to appear dishonest, or a timid witness cowed.

The damage done to the opposing witness in cross-examination would pose no troublesome dilemma for the lawyer if the true facts were known with certainty, but seldom does a lawyer know the precise boundaries of the truth in a particular case. Take a car wreck case in which witnesses differ as to the speed of the cars or the color of the stoplight. The lawyer can only make educated guesses as to which version is closer to the truth. If a breach of contract case depends on conflicting recollections of the precise statements made during negotiation of the contract, the lawyer will not know for certain which side is right. So it goes in most cases. The lawyer may suspect or even strongly believe that a witness is lying or mistaken, including the lawyer's own client. But the lawyer's clear duty is to balance all doubts in favor of the client, to seek to advance the version of conflicting stories most favorable to that client.

The cross-examination of a crucial witness in trial by a skillful advocate can be the closest that person might ever come to the experience of torture on the rack. With no chance to escape, and with many others watching, a witness is required to answer questions framed by a highly trained professional who may, if circumstances warrant, be bent on destruction.

Unlike an actual torturer, the cross-examiner is not necessarily aiming at the extraction of a confession. One need not utter the words of guilt to be made to appear guilty in court. A lie can often be exposed more forcefully when it is denied than when admitted. A jury's most vehement fury is often reserved for those who tenaciously cling to a falsehood, or who make incredible protestations of innocence.

A cross-examination considered successful by the lawyer can be excruciatingly painful or humiliating for the witness, whether deservedly so or not. I have seen parties to lawsuits forsake their claim entirely or settle for far less than they might have won in court, just to avoid the ordeal of cross-examination, even when they know their testimony will be truthful. To the hapless witness, the cross-examiner is seen not merely as advocate for the other side, but as persecutor. Meanwhile, the lawyer inflicting this pain is only fulfilling an ethical duty. This leads me to another teaching of life after law school:

LESSON TWO: *Law is the only learned profession in which one is ethically obligated to hurt people.*

The lawyer's duty of zealous advocacy extends to all clients, guilty or innocent, rich or poor, saint or psychopath. The ax murderer is ethically entitled to the same devotion of purpose as Mother Teresa. If it happens that a person who is the modern-day George Washington of truth-tellers becomes the key witness against an advocate's client, the lawyer still has the same obligation to seek "zealously" to disparage, cast doubt upon, or even destroy him. The helping mandate of the legal profession enshrines the principle of an essentially amoral dedication to obtain the best possible outcome for the client, even at the risk of hurting a more deserving adversary.

One need not be in the battleground of trial, however, to wield the painful sword of the advocate. In virtually every form of adversarial lawyering, in or out of court, this helping/hurting dynamic arises. As negotiator or advisor, the lawyer has the same duty to advance the client's position as far as possible without violating the law, whatever the impact upon other people.

Consider a hypothetical claim brought by an inexperienced lawyer on behalf of the widow of a man killed in an automobile accident. The driver of the other car, though totally at fault, is uninsured. The woman's sole hope to recover money for her husband's death is under his own insurance policies. At the time of the fatal accident, her husband ran a small business and owned two cars. His business and both cars were insured by Grasping Hands Insurance Company.

In his inexperience, the widow's lawyer does not realize that recent court decisions dealing with the "stacking" of insurance policies permit recovery of up to $100,000 on the business policy *plus* $50,000 on each of the two auto policies. Accordingly, he seeks an out-of-court settlement for only the $50,000 death benefit limits on the car involved in the accident. Seeing the young lawyer's mistake, the lawyer for Grasping Hands quickly agrees to settle for $50,000 in exchange for a binding release of all claims against his client.

Because the insurance company's lawyer is well aware of the law, he also knows the settlement is unjust to the widow, yet he seizes the opportunity to benefit his client. As long as no fraud or other legal violation is involved, a lawyer in this situation is not only permitted but *ethically obligated* to strike the best deal possible for his or her client, whether it is just or not.

Sooner or later in every lawyer's life, the time comes when, looking back over a successfully concluded case, he or she realizes that the scales of justice were tipped decisively by the imbalance in the skills of the opposing lawyers. The impact of this realization is alternately thrilling and chilling. The professional pride in obtaining a great result for a client brings the thrill; the chill comes with the recognition that the other side would have won if the clients had switched lawyers.

A sage trial lawyer was once asked whether, throughout the course of his long career, he thought justice was done to his clients. He replied: "When I was younger, I lost some cases I should have won. When I was older, I won some cases I should have lost. In the long run, it all evened out. On balance, justice was done." This oft-told tale of lawyering captures the exquisite frustration of the advocate facing the reality that neither bungling nor brilliant lawyering equates with justice. As one cynical trial lawyer colleague recently put it, "In law school I was taught that justice is the highest aim of jurisprudence, but after 25 years, I've determined that justice is a happy client."

In fact, when experienced lawyers get together over drinks to tell war stories, the courtroom tales most lauded often show the widest divergence between result and justice—the obviously guilty client who is acquitted by a stirring closing argument; the malingering personal injury claimant who recovers a bundle from a large corporation; the conviction of a criminal defendant on the slimmest imaginable evidence. The skilled advocates whose forensic exploits obtain these unjust ends, using ethically permissible talents and tactics, are glorified within the profession.

COROLLARY TO LESSON TWO: *The more able and experienced a lawyer, the greater the chance that he or she will achieve a miscarriage of justice.*

Another conundrum of adversarial ethics is created when a morally repulsive client seeks counsel.

Several years ago, a highly respected trial lawyer whose practice consisted mainly of representing reputable businesses in lawsuits received a phone call from a friend and suburban neighbor, who tensely reported that he was calling from jail and urgently needed advice. Dropping everything, the lawyer rushed to the jail, where he found that his friend had been arrested on a morals charge: flashing his privates to passersby in a public park. Upon learning that his neighbor admitted the acts, the shocked lawyer delivered a brief righteous sermon along the lines of: "How could you do such a disgusting thing? Look at the position you've put you're family in. More importantly, my own children might have seen you. Since you admit to these revolting acts, I have no intention of trying to get you off these valid charges." Whereupon the lawyer indignantly stomped out of jail.

The suburban flasher was immediately plunged into a near-suicidal state of despondency. Thumbing through the jail house phone book, trying to stifle overwhelming feelings of guilt and remorse, he called a criminal lawyer listed in the Yellow Pages. The lawyer who responded to his call was also repulsed by the man's conduct, but he undertook the case, ultimately managing to negotiate a plea bargain that entailed payment of a fine, psychological treatment, and a period of supervised probation.

In dealing with the suburban flasher, which lawyer acted ethically? Some would argue that refusal to represent an admittedly guilty client on a repulsive criminal charge is quintessentially ethical. The fundamental moral principle is: I will not further your moral wrongdoing through use of my talents on your behalf. But in the context of legal ethics, only the lawyer who represented the guilty person zealously and nonjudgmentally fulfilled the aspirations of the profession.

The very core of American legal ethics authorizes—some might even say the glorifies—the representation of a client whose conduct one finds unlawful, injurious or morally offensive. To those outside the profession, the lawyer's stance seems irredeemably duplicitous. The very idea of being an advocate for the guilty seems wrong to most people.

Nor is this quandary of the advocate limited to the practice of criminal law. Given the litigation clientele of even the most respectable law firms these days, virtually all trial lawyers wear the moral millstone of arguing successfully for a wrongdoer with some regularity. The dishonest business promoter whose lawyer persuades consumer protection authorities to back off their investigation is freed to mulct more victims. A quiet settlement with the most vocal complainants against a loan-sharking finance company can buy time for more unlawful loans to be collected. The sexual harasser with a good lawyer may succeed in disparaging the initial victim, enabling the pattern of harassment to continue. In these and countless other instances, innocent people may be harmed as a direct consequence of the lawyer's zealous, completely ethical, representation.

The obligations imposed by legal ethics inevitably cause the lawyer's behavior to diverge on some occasions from personal morality. Good lawyers sometimes further the causes of bad people and ethical lawyers sometimes hurt good people. This divergence between legal and personal ethics helps to explain the gulf between the public's perception of conniving and immoral lawyers and the fact that lawyers discipline their ranks better than any other profession in history.

Can lawyers avoid the burdens of the advocate's role by aspiring to a higher standard of conduct than that prescribed by the lawyers' code of ethics? Especially since the 1960's, significant numbers of determined and idealistic law students have vowed to rise above the edicts of a profession they view as charging them to carry the legal banners of the unworthy. Committed to social justice, they have pledged not to represent polluters, sexists, oppressors, racists, and so on. On the level of personal morality, they have vowed not to advance unjust causes, not to take advantage of inexperienced or unskilled opponents, and not to represent those with whom they disagree, let alone whom they detest.

In reality, however, rare is the lawyer who can escape the burden of the advocate's duty to hurt. A friend who is a committed environmental lawyer once described a personal moral dilemma he faced after resolving only to represent clients whom he believed would advance the cause of preserving the environment. After considerable reading and research, he had consented to represent a company that proposed to build a huge incinerator for the disposal of solid wastes. The lawyer was convinced that the environment would be enhanced by recycling some waste materials and efficiently burning those that couldn't be recycled.

A protracted legal proceeding ensued, in which scientists, using both old and newly emerging scientific theories, dissected the incinerator proposal. Midway in the engagement, my friend concluded that new evidence showed that the incinerator was a worse polluter than other forms of waste disposal, that his initial conclusion had been wrong, and that he was representing the "wrong" side.

The rules of legal ethics regarding the withdrawal of a lawyer from a pending lawsuit do not permit a lawyer to withdraw from a case for a mere disagreement with the client's position. A lawyer cannot fire a client simply because the client's stance is viewed by the lawyer as morally unjust. Even an environmental idealist can find himself ethically required to use his considerable talents to achieve a result he has come to believe would worsen the environment, and this is exactly what my friend did.

Some lawyers believe they can ease the moral burden of advocacy by limiting their clientele to certain types of people, such as the poor or the disadvantaged. In short order, they learn that membership in an underprivileged group does not assure the justness of an individual's case. They soon encounter a poor client who is lying in order to avoid paying rent, or discover that another's accusation of racism is invented or grossly exaggerated. Suddenly, they must grapple with the tension between fidelity to client and to justice that only an ideologue with blinders can ignore. No one can always select clients with any degree of accuracy who always deserve to win, or whose cause ultimately will prove to be just. Every lawyer will sooner or later feel the weight of the ethical compulsion to advance a detested cause, to hurt someone who does not deserve to be hurt.

Lawyers go to great lengths to rationalize this hurtful side of their role in administering justice. Their justifications, or denials, seem to fall into two main categories: the opponents deserved what they got; and the give-and-take of the adversary system causes justice to emerge from conflicting positions.

Lawyers can almost always convince themselves that the other side deserved to lose or to gain a less favorable settlement. A cunning trial lawyer who has just persuaded a jury to render an unjust verdict favorable to his or her client will often point to the generous settlement offer that the other side rejected before trial. You see, they have no one but themselves to blame, the lawyer smugly exults. They should have realized the risks of trial. They decided to roll the dice and they lost. Absent in the lawyer's euphoria of self-congratulation is any reflective consideration of who truly deserved to win the case.

Most lawyers avert their focus from the hurtful side of lawyering with the simple rationalization that the system requires their conduct. Justice emerges, the argument goes, from good lawyers hammering hard for opposing clients' causes, from the marketplace of competing ideas. It often does, just as peace follows from killing in war. But the fact that the system works does not lift the personal burden of serving as an instrument of hurt and pain from the soldier— or from the lawyer.

# CHAPTER THREE

# Law School's Best-Forgotten Lessons

P BS listeners who are fans of Garrison Keillor's radio show, *A Prairie Home Companion*, will have a sense of my midwestern milieu as a liberal arts student at the University of Minnesota in the mid-1960's. Keillor and I were classmates, if that term fits in a University community of 50,000 students and faculty. He was already publishing brilliant literary pieces as editor of *The Ivory Tower*, the campus literary magazine, and in *The Minnesota Daily*, the campus newspaper. Though I was student body president and we both graduated in the same year, 1966, Keillor and I never met. Yet it is evident from his folksy radio monologues set in Lake Wobegon that we were both products of the same heartland culture of the period before optimistic student ferment for social change became transformed by the Vietnam War into a sullen rejection of all authority.

Our favorite son in Minnesota politics was Vice President Hubert Horatio Humphrey, the "Happy Warrior," the man who had brought the visage of midwestern socialism with a smile to the U. S. Senate. At the time of my graduation, anti-war protests took the form of "teach-ins," rather than students strikes or bombings. We still sought to influence leaders, not to dispense with all of them. Reasoned opposition discourse had not yet given way to "Dump the Hump" placards attacking our very own Vice President.

Our university professors subscribed to a teaching style consistent with what has since been termed "Minnesota Nice"; even those who were expansive and intellectually probing were also adherents of personally non-confrontive learning in a form that New Yorkers find smarmy, naive, and superficial, but which has deep roots in Minnesota's strangely blended heritage of prairie populists and Norwegian Lutherans. Deep down, we Minnesotans of the mid-'60's, including even college professors and students, were all from Lake Wobegon, where "all the children are above average."

Nothing in my Minnesota background prepared me for Mr. G.D.G. Hall and my first few tutorials as a law student at Exeter College, Oxford, where I went in 1966 as a Rhodes Scholar. Gone instantly was the comfortable anonymity of a large university classroom. It was just G.D.G. and I, one-on-one for an interminable hour per week, he dressed in English tweeds while I wore the required black Oxford scholar's gown. He puffed on a pipe in his book-ringed college lodgings that doubled as our tutorial setting, while I slumped no more than five feet away in an overstuffed chair, reading aloud my assigned essay on a topic in the law of torts. Also gone was any semblance of Minnesota Nice. With very few exceptions, G.D.G. didn't care for Americans, and I soon learned I clearly was not one of the favored few. Even with English students, G.D.G. believed that droll ridicule was the paragon of pedagogy, an approach that rose to an art form when he was instructing Americans.

Professor Hall began each tutorial amiably enough, with ostensibly good-natured chit-chat unrelated to the law. A typical opening gambit might deal with library hours. As an early riser, he once said, he found the American habit of early library opening hours preferable to the later English habits. He smiled to put me at ease. He joked about English food or unheated college rooms. When I was fully relaxed and slouched comfortably in my chair, he nudged the discussion into the subject of the week's essay, an arcane topic like "Does *Rylands v. Fletcher* still govern the [English] law of strict liability?" or a sweeping survey assignment like "Discuss the English law of nuisance."

Sometimes before the essay-reading began, but always before it had proceeded far, the tone of the tutorial took an abrupt turn. One way or another, G.D.G. managed to shatter the room's relaxed atmosphere with an acidic verbal sledgehammer. The turning point might be as insignificant as my mispronunciation of the name of a British brewery in a case (Does Ind Coope have a long or short "I"?) or as weighty as forgetting a fact in a case on the week's designated reading list. Inevitably, as soon as my guard was down from the initial affable bantering, G.D.G. transformed the educational approach in that medieval college room from Minnesota Nice to English Derision. Needless to say, there was plenty to ridicule in my essays, for I had not studied law before and was unfamiliar with the process of "thinking like a lawyer" that is the main skill imparted in law school.

A few weeks into our tutorials, G.D.G. had me pegged academically. With a grave finality, he pronounced that I was destined, no matter how hard I studied, to be a "beta, not an alpha" student. (I should have known to be more distrustful of a college grading system that doesn't even use the letters of its native tongue.) For him, this assessment was not just a reflection of the quality of my work to that point, but a permanently-etched declaration of my inherent intellectual limitations. For G.D.G., in a quintessentially English fashion, my place in the academic hierarchy was as perpetually fixed as a Cockney's social standing in London.

Not until I saw the movie *The Paper Chase* years later did I realize the close similarities between my Oxford exposure to the study of law with G.D.G. and the teaching style of American legal education in vogue until about the late '60's. I don't think I ever identified more viscerally with the predicament of a fictional character than I did with the first-year Harvard Law School student in that film, who is motivated to excel academically by his raw hatred of the respected but dreaded Professor Kingsfield, another teacher who subscribed to the learn-by-ridicule approach. Despite his stature and keen intellect, Kingsfield would never have been elected to the school board in Lake Wobegon.

We like to think we have left behind the Socratic sarcasm that typified the law school teaching of most American lawyers who are 45 or older, but I doubt that the changes have been as great as the law schools proclaim. Overt belittling in class may no longer be the rule, but strong evidence suggests that the study of law today evokes the same reaction in many students as G.D.G. did in me.

More than at any other time in my 21 years of formal education, I reacted to Hall's approach with something akin to, if not clinically defined as, depression. I accepted much of his ridicule as being deserved, at least to the extent that I saw myself at that time as less accomplished than others in the skills of legal analysis. My sense of self-worth plummeted, I became despondent and angry at my own ineptitude, and I seriously pondered whether I was cut out for a career in law at all.

Not a depression-prone person, I managed to rebound from that first ego-crushing term of Oxford tutorials. With the help of a younger and more sympathetic tutor in the winter term and with the assistance of my English student peers, I began to make strides in writing better essays and in deciphering English legal cases. By my second year at Oxford, I was defying G.D.G.'s prognosis and doing some "alpha" work.

When I was again assigned to Hall during that second year for a series of tutorials in his particular area of expertise, English legal history, I even had a moment of *Paper Chase*-type triumph. Paying me the ultimate compliment that can be accorded a student by an Oxford don, he asked me to give him a copy of one of my tutorial essays written on an esoteric topic. I, who have trouble remembering what I received for Christmas last year, will never forget that the essay dealt with *Slade's Case*, a seminal 17th Century decision. The clearest measure of the distance I had traveled from Lake Wobegon was my curt refusal to do so. In my best deadpan imitation of his professorial style, I replied,

"What possible use could you have for the writing of a beta-level student?"

Looking back with more than a 25-year perspective on this exchange, I still marvel at how petulant and out of character my response was. In the Minnesota of my background, I would never have contemplated such a snide retort. I think I needed a measure of personal vindication, peevish or not, to convince myself that I had risen above the pit of my first-year depression.

I suppose I should credit G.D.G. Hall for providing me with valuable lessons that served me well in my later life in the courtroom. In ways I almost regret to acknowledge, his tutorial hazings prepared me for encounters with belittling judges or sarcastic adversaries. I also may have been motivated to study harder than otherwise to pull myself above the level to which he had pegged me. But I find even now that I can extend gratitude to Hall only in the same sense that the 95-pound weakling of the comic book ads of my childhood, though now bulging with muscles acquired through the Charles Atlas body-building program, might thank the bully who first kicked sand in his face.

Despite my survival of the Hall tutorials with no lasting injury to self-esteem, the fact that my closest brush with the depressive abyss occurred during my first year of studying law must hold a kernel of meaning beyond mere coincidence. Reading the most authoritative studies of the psychological impacts of the law school years on American students has since convinced me that my Oxford ordeal was far more typical than I had supposed.

An overall average of 3%-9% of people living in the world's industrial nations suffer from depression. Yet the best scientific studies have shown that the incidence of depression in law students jumps to an astounding 17%-40%. When these data were first published in the 1970's, some questioned their meaning, arguing, alternatively, that law students may be predisposed towards depression, or that any psychologically stressful impact of law school was temporary in nature.

Yet follow-up studies in the 1980's conducted on students before, during, and two years after law school have concluded that students entering law schools show no more signs of depressive tendencies than does the general population. So much for the predisposition theory.

At the other end, young lawyers studied after law school manifest the same pattern of a highly elevated incidence of depression as do first year students. Something of disturbing psychological dimensions happens when otherwise relatively normal people start studying law, and the effects appear to be lasting even beyond law school.

What causes the heightened psychological distress of so many law students? Two obvious candidates—the heavy workload and financial pressures fed by mounting indebtedness—contribute to a certain extent to stress levels. But students of that other expensive and work-driven profession, medicine, do not show the same remarkable upswing in depression during medical school that plagues law students. We must, I think, look for causes more in the unique attributes of legal education itself and in the conditions shaping the lives of lawyers.

So what are the common threads that tie my experience to that of all law students? What plunges so many into depression? Far more than a personality clash with a professor or intimidating teaching style contributed to my deep malaise as a beginning law student. That realization brings me to one of the lessons untaught in law school:

LESSON THREE: *Law school depresses students through gloomy immersion in the risks of life, the glorification of dispute, and a process of moral neutering.*

The hallmark of both the American and English approaches to legal education is the case study method. Instead of reading legal codes, textbooks or treatises by scholars, students learn the principles of law by carefully reading and discussing actual cases. The cases in law school casebooks are selected less for the brilliance of the judges who decided them or even for the correctness of their analysis than for their utility to provoke debate and discussion. The emphasis is not so much on acquiring knowledge of the law as on learning how to understand and analyze legal problems.

During my first weeks at Oxford under Professor Hall's tutelage, I read English torts cases. A course in torts is a major part of the first year curriculum in American law schools as well. As an enthusiastic new law student, I immersed myself in the human stories revealed by these tort cases: the case of the woman who was innocently walking down a village lane when a large limb broke off a homeowner's tree, badly maiming her; the case about the well-trained and long-docile circus elephant that went inexplicably berserk, injuring a circus-goer. Day after day, I read all about the various mishaps by which people can suffer injury: train wrecks, runaway trucks, slipping on a spot of ice cream, and so on. All law students remember their own litany of human tragedy.

For me, as for many law students, the focused study of torts cases was a perspective-changing experience. Emerging from the law library, I found myself glancing at overhanging limbs, which suddenly loomed with a more sinister shadow. Crossing the street, I took several extra looks to be sure no runaway truck was plunging down the hill. Everyday objects, such as soda cans, suddenly had the potential to explode on contact. In short, the whole world was fraught with a multitude of risks of which I now had a keenly heightened awareness. No human activity, not even going to the circus, was exempt from the potential for grave disaster.

Although that initial overdose of tort student risk aversion subsided quickly, I was changed forever, whether I liked it or not. Never again could I ride a simple carnival amusement ride without thinking that the person who welded the seat mountings to the Ferris wheel was probably getting the minimum wage for his efforts, and that each weld was the only barrier between me and grievous injury.

The study of torts, like the study of all types of legal cases, is necessarily an over-exposure to the graphic and ever-present risks of living. It is the lawyer's role, after all, to anticipate and contend with the consequences of those risks. The first teaching of law school, therefore, is to approach life with greater apprehension, with a heightened sense of all that can go wrong. A legal education dampens the spirits of the bold and can virtually paralyze those already disposed to be cautious.

Other first-year law courses also focus on human misfortune, if in a less dramatic fashion. The study of contract cases is largely an analysis of deals gone sour. Criminal law emphasizes not only deviant social behavior but also the worst excesses of police and prosecutors. Whatever the subject, law school glimpses of it tend to be skewed towards the dismal. Even to a student infused with enthusiasm, the vision of humanity presented in law school case books is hardly uplifting. The staunchest optimist has difficulty coming through the law school years without a more negative view of the world. It's not surprising that the subject matter of legal case books would shove some students—particularly those imbued with youthful idealism—closer to depression.

Anyone who has had a spouse, sibling, friend, or child go through law school needs no convincing as to the second point—that a legal education instills greater disputatiousness. The process of learning to "think like a lawyer" is fundamentally the development of a critical skepticism about any proposition, no matter how seemingly straightforward. A single seemingly unassailable phrase from a legal case may be the subject of an entire hour of a law school class, with the professor posing question after question to test the application of the legal principle to different cases.

Take a holding of a simple case, such as the mundane idea that a letter sent through the U.S. mails is presumed to have been received. Any law professor worth his or her salt could spend an entire class probing the reach of that rule, with questions such as: "What if a natural calamity, such as an earthquake or fire, casts doubt on the mail delivery? What if the recipient has moved: does the presumption include forwarding? What if the recipient is in an institution, like a hospital or college dorm, where mail is handled by non-postal employees before it reaches the recipient? Does the presumption apply if the recipient is known by the sender to be temporarily insane or incapacitated?"

You get the idea. Almost any rule or concept, no matter how sensible in general, is subject to attack when applied in every conceivable context. More than anything else, law school teaches the ability to dispute virtually anything. If I learned nothing else from him, Professor Hall taught me that I could not utter two successive paragraphs even in informal discourse without exposing myself to his ridiculing attack. As first-year law students in America also discover, nothing in their previous lives has prepared them for the inherently deflating and terrifyingly intimidating exercise of opening their mouths in a law school classroom. No matter how gentle the professor's style, the initial process of learning to think in public with unnatural rigor is almost always humiliating.

Moreover, the use of this new-found analytical skill in ordinary conversations can drive friends of law students crazy. We tend to lead our day-to-day lives by acting on simple notions without much conscious thought. A letter sent is presumed received. The circus is a safe place to be. Leave it to a law student, however, to divert an offhand comment into a fifteen-minute argument about the ways the mail can be waylaid or injuries suffered at the circus.

Nor is this tendency of law students towards gratuitous disputation merely a trivial irritant. What to the student is essentially an analytical mind exercise is often received by the listener as a personally aggressive verbal assault, or at least a coldly distancing diversion. Many a law student's friendship or even marriage has foundered over this issue, with the unhappy friend or spouse saying, "Why can't we just carry on a normal conversation as we did before law school? Why do we always have to argue about everything?"

Even if a law student's relationships survive, the interpersonal setbacks are sometimes sufficient to plunge one into depression. After loss of friends or spouse at a time when they are most needed, only Prozac may offer relief.

Besides risk immersion and hair-trigger argumentativeness, law school's third main impact derives from learning the lawyer's role as advocate. Simply put, law school seeks to enshrine the virtue of the professional advocate who zealously furthers the cause of even a morally abhorred client. The message obviously is not this overt. But the underlying highest value taught, even if implicitly, is the ability to come up with convincing reasons in support of any argument, whether one personally agrees with them or not, and to defend those reasons with cogent and convincing logic, on behalf of anybody.

In a law school discussion of the topic of abortion, for example, the focus will inevitably be upon legal doctrines. *Roe v. Wade* is, after all, an interpretation of the U.S. Constitution. Law students who seek to advance their arguments by religious, social, or moral arguments on either side of the issue may find themselves facing the withering inquiries of a professor forcing them to mold their sentiments into a legal analysis: "You may agree or disagree with the outcome of *Roe v. Wade,* but how does it rate as an exercise of legal logic?" "Is it the right holding for the wrong reasons?" "If so, what other reasons would you, as judge, use?" "Is the medical portion of the case still scientifically valid?" "If not, does that undermine the decision?" And so on.

It is through this process that law students, in order to perform well, tend to become morally neutered. The moral decision to act or not act—to legalize abortion or not, for example—becomes far less important than the reasoning process that attends it. The right result is valued less than the right analysis. Step by step, law students are distanced from personal values, from the very precept that such values are paramount.

Paradoxically, some law professors these days attempt to substitute a version of political correctness for lost personal morality, which subjects students to a kind of double whammy. First, they are strip-searched and deprived of their individual moral compasses by the glorification of the ideal of the professional advocate. And second, they are led to believe that only a result-oriented system that fosters the ends of a particular social or political agenda is morally correct.

It took me only a year or two of law practice in the real world to unlearn the most distorting effects of my legal education, to realize that even finely-tuned legal stratagems must be harmonized with common sense, and to appreciate that the neutering of values in the realm of legal advocacy cannot serve as a guide to the rest of one's life. I can't imagine how long it will take today's students.

CHAPTER FOUR

# The Thrill of Victory, the Agony of Defeat, and the Other 99% of Your Life

An aspiring trial lawyer picturing him or herself arguing brilliantly to a jury in a courtroom might better
dream again.

The single most glaring deception perpetrated by every
movie and TV show about law practice, from *Perry Mason*
to *L. A. Law*, is to ignore the utter and crushing tedium of
much of the work. The false perception that legal disputes
move smoothly and swiftly from initial client interview to
trial, or even the very notion that the case will ever be decided by a jury, communicates an unreal picture of the
lawyer's life.

Never before in the course of American history have so
many lawyers done so much work for so few trials.

With a few exceptions, it has become almost a rare occurrence for trial lawyers to try cases. A small minority of lawyers
in certain areas of governmental practice, such as prosecu-

tors, public defenders, or child abuse advocates, have the chance to use and hone their trial skills on a reasonably regular basis. Some personal injury lawyers who handle a large case volume, whether on the plaintiff's side or for insurance companies, can be assured of trial experience. Divorce lawyers, too, get to try some cases, though typically not to a jury. Even in these more litigious fields, however, fewer cases, proportionally speaking, are tried in most parts of the country than was the case forty or even twenty years ago.

There remain some shrinking regional pockets sprinkled throughout America, most often in the dwindling rural areas, where judges still believe that even the parties to a civil dispute deserve their day in court. In some of the country courthouses of agrarian outstate Minnesota, judges adhere to the idea that benefits flow from the display of justice in action through public trials. Lawyers who practice in those areas have trial opportunities largely unavailable elsewhere.

But, for the first time in more than 200 years of American jurisprudence, the majority of judges now believe that a jury trial of a civil case represents a failure of the modern "system for administration of justice." If the parties have not become exhausted by delay, procedural burdens, and interminable pre-trial investigation of the claim; if they have not been diverted from the judicial system by cajoling towards mediation, arbitration, or some other form of "alternative dispute resolution"; if their wallets have not yet been emptied by litigation costs, litigants are likely to be in for a rude awakening when their case is finally called for trial. These days, the "trial judge" is likely to employ a variety of devices, ranging from principled jawboning to outright coercion, to discourage the parties from submitting their disputes to a jury.

Not long ago, a large civil case in my community laboriously wended its way through the various pre-trial impediments and was finally called for trial. Both sides were well represented by capable lawyers. They had attempted to settle the case, but the differences between the parties were seemingly irreconcilable. Everyone held steadfast as the judge went through his litany of arguments as to why the case should be settled rather than tried. Jury selection had actually begun when the lead lawyer for the defense collapsed with a stroke and died in the courtroom. Faced with this extraordinary turn of events, both sides readily agreed that a short continuance of the case was in order to permit a new lawyer to prepare to present evidence.

The judge, showing a sensitivity akin to Ghengis Khan, took the parties and their lawyers aside separately to discuss the future of the case. To the defense and its new lead lawyer, the judge announced that he was inclined to deny the request for a delay of the trial. In the interim, he strongly urged the parties to make one last effort to settle their differences. As the new lead lawyer for the defense could not possibly be ready to try such a complicated case properly without additional time for preparation, the judge's message was clear: if no settlement was achieved, the defense would suffer in court.

Next the judge spoke privately to the plaintiff's side, which desperately wanted the litigation saga to come to an end as quickly as possible. He had a very busy trial calendar for months to come, he told them, and was therefore inclined to postpone the trial for a year or more. Settlement surely seemed a better alternative than such a postponement of justice, the judge intoned. The plaintiff, he intimated, would sorely regret any failure to settle the case.

In the wee hours of the next morning, following extended and feverish settlement negotiations, the two sides discovered that they had been coerced to come to the bargaining table by diametrically opposite threats. This realization evoked such visceral disgust at the legal system that the parties finally reached consensus on one issue, at least: that as much as they disliked each other and felt they each deserved to win, no disagreement should be entrusted to a judge capable of such duplicity. Motivated by this mutual spirit of aversion, they arrived at terms for settlement.

One old settlement-inducing bromide that judges never tire of repeating is that the best settlement is one that leaves both sides unhappy. While this expression contains a kernel of truth when applied to many bitter litigants who would be better off burying their hatchets, it becomes perverted where the impetus to settle is fear, the fear of presenting the dispute to a wrathful judge who broadly hints at injudicious treatment for any party deemed to be recalcitrant in the settlement process. An agreement coerced by threat of unjust treatment is not unlike a tortured confession: it may be right, but the process leaves no one believing the interests of justice were served.

Savvy insurance company lawyers have learned to hold back most of their settlement dollars until after the now-customary pre-trial settlement lecture by the judge, which permits them to appear generous before an arm-twisting jurist. Thus, the net effect of the behavior of the most settlement-happy judges can be to defer meaningful negotiations until the very last stage of the litigation, leading to both delays in resolving cases and greatly heightened pre-trial costs. For lawyers, the impact is that far more time is spent maneuvering the case into a position for settlement on the courthouse steps, and far less time in trial.

Because of this bias towards settlement of lawsuits, the odds of a young lawyer trying a jury case within the first two years of practice for a major law firm are now lower than the chances of being hit by lightning while commuting to work. The smaller cases typically assigned to new lawyers are the ones most likely to be pressured into settlement by a judge who reasons that a $15,000 dispute is "not worth the court's time."

Nor is the lack of courtroom exposure limited to younger lawyers. For perhaps the first time in the history of American advocacy, it is common even for experienced trial lawyers to have gaps of several years between trials. Large law firms frequently promote trial lawyers to the partnership who have never litigated a case to verdict before a jury.

Ironically, the brightest lawyers who handle the biggest civil cases often have minimal courtroom experience, an aberrant reality that can muck up the works of the wheels of justice. Lawyers unaccustomed to the courtroom tend to be discomfited by the relatively unpredictable environment of a jury trial. They can overlook the human elements of a case, like the jury appeal of a particular witness. They can fail to anticipate the emotional arguments that count for nothing in law school but amount to everything in trial. I have heard brilliant lawyers who, sensing at least on some level the true extent of their lack of trial experience and the handicap that presents, express apprehension and downright fear of the very idea of going to trial.

Whatever the causes, it does not take a statistical wizard to make calculations and graph the trials-per-lawyer numbers. In many urban areas, fewer civil cases are being tried today in absolute terms than twenty years ago, while the ranks of lawyers handling such cases have quadrupled over the same period.

If more and more lawyers are trying fewer and fewer cases, what does that mean for those who call themselves trial lawyers?

LESSON FOUR: *In modern litigation, as in trench warfare, most of the time is spent digging the trenches.*

The stuff of litigation today is not trials, but discovery, legal research, motions, and maneuvering.

The discovery phase of a lawsuit begins with a sense of excitement and anticipation. The rules of discovery were designed to permit each side, in an above-board, orderly fashion, to investigate the facts underlying the case before going to trial. In discovery, each side may gain access to all of the documents relating to the case, such as medical records, pertinent correspondence, or business diaries. The proverbial "smoking gun" evidence is sometimes "discovered" by this means.

By taking depositions—out-of-court questioning of the other party or witnesses under oath—lawyers not only get answers to crucial questions, but also can observe the mannerisms and appearance of the cast of lawsuit characters.

Rounding out the lawyer's tools of discovery are inter-rogatories, formal written questions that must be answered by the adversary under oath, which are especially useful to get essential tidbits of information like the dates of events or names and addresses of witnesses.

Collectively, these procedures are supposed to expedite the lawyers' fact-finding search, encourage settlement of disputes, and lessen the perversities of justice caused by nasty surprises in the courtroom. The discovery rules, it is said, prevent trial by ambush and, properly applied, they work.

But all too often, the discovery phase of a lawsuit be-comes like a Pac-Man mouth, voraciously gobbling up the entire litigation in monstrously costly and tedious proce-dures. Vast quantities of marginally relevant documents are requested from both sides, in the hope that the evidentiary golden needle will be found in a haystack of paper. Deposi-tions drag on not merely for hours but for days, during which the parties are worn down physically, hazed emotionally, and depleted financially. One of my clients endured a mara-thon deposition for a total of thirteen days. The mountains of documents produced during a lawsuit must all be re-viewed. The lawyers in a case must prepare for and attend all depositions, no matter how plodding or trivial.

While many factors contribute to the excesses of discov-ery, judicial discouragement of trials and the lack of trial experience of lawyers are high on the list. As the prospect of a trial becomes a more remote likelihood, a lawyer correctly reasons that the only remaining avenue to score points in settlement posturing is through the discovery process, and the lawyer who fears the courtroom is far more likely to extend discovery in the hope of wearing down the opposition or stumbling upon the elusive key fact that will give his or her side the stronger hand in settlement.

Because of the burdens of discovery, the victor in a lawsuit is often determined more by the psychic and financial stamina of the parties than by the merits of the case. Litigants settle as much from sheer exhaustion from discovery as from the facts they have discovered.

From the client's point of view, at least the discovery process is visible. Clients can examine the important documents obtained from the opponent or watch the defendant squirm during a deposition. However costly and slow-paced these procedures may be, they usually cause the litigation trench to be dug an inch closer to the besieged adversary's fortress.

In contrast, clients are befuddled at the role of legal research and motions in a lawsuit. A litigant may have carefully selected a lawyer with a reputation for being knowledgeable in the field of the client's case, such as employment law, labor law, or securities law. When that same client receives a detailed itemized monthly billing from the lawyer, he or she is often shocked to see large chunks of very expensive legal time devoted to "legal research." Typical first reactions to such bills are "I'm not about to pay you for your legal education!" or "I hired you because I thought you knew the law, why are you charging me for looking it up?"

More than ever before, the cost of litigation reflects the many hours of legal research needed to be certain that all of the law pertinent to a case has been located and analyzed. This phenomenon is not the result of any shortcoming of the nation's law schools; nor would extra years of legal education reduce it. Only a small proportion of legal research is driven by the impulse that promotes duplicative or marginally necessary testing within the medical profession: fear of malpractice lawsuits.

Rather, the higher costs for legal research time are more indicative of the advanced level of training and ability of lawyers than the absence of those skills. Computer-wise law graduates with superb research talents, using staggeringly vast data bases available through Lexis and other on-line services, can now conduct rapid searches through the statutes and cases of all fifty states to locate the legal authorities most similar to any given client's dispute.

Consider, for example, a case in which a child who has been skateboarding on a residential street has been injured after being hit by a car. At first blush, the principles of the general law of negligence would seem to apply to the case, and a seasoned litigator would see little if any benefit from conducting much research. Indeed, old-style legal research, based on manual review and reading of cases, would probably not be worth the effort. Aside from a quick glance at recent cases from the state where the case arose, any effort to access the millions of pages of cases from other states would be a waste of the client's money.

But the accessibility of every American legal decision by computer now makes a search for applicable cases not only possible but necessary. Simply by instructing the computer to search for the word "skateboard," one is likely to find some case, somewhere, in which an appeals judge pronounced learned words, say on the subject of skateboarding on a public street, words you may wish to quote during your case, or words your opponent will no doubt quote and for which you will need a convincing reply, preferably in the form of a contrary decision by another judge.

Should a contract dispute turn on the interpretation of a few words in the contract, the computer can find every printed decision in which a court has contemplated those very same words, a feat that was once virtually impossible even if one could manually pore over the thousands of potentially relevant cases.

While the computer aids lawyers enormously, the extra cases it now locates must be analyzed and responded to using traditional legal writing methods that are only marginally enhanced by computer technology. The raw materials for the lawyer's briefs may pop up in electronic milliseconds, but analysis and writing go forth using a real-time mind. The ability to find more law more quickly thus expands the total time spent on legal research and writing and increases the billings to the client. For the lawyer, this change represents a shift in workload: more time is spent in the law library and in legal writing relative to time spent in court.

But the impact of the computer is only one part of the overall rise in time spent researching and writing about the law. Another significant factor is the snowballing increase in the volume of the law. Appeals court judges, who write the published opinions that form the basis for legal research, are writing longer and longer decisions. The law is more complex, judges are better trained, and appeals court judges all have intelligent law clerks who have the eagerness and time to prepare lengthy draft opinions.

Legislators and government bureaucrats are churning out new statutes and regulations at an ever-increasing rate, all of which provide grist for the legal interpretation mill. And almost every year new courts are created, such as specialty administrative tribunals to interpret governmental regulations or intermediate or specialty state appeals courts, that spew out an ever-expanding volume of legal decisions to be researched and analyzed.

No longer do students go to law school to learn the law. The body of law in America is far too vast for any human being to learn. Instead, law students learn how to *find* the law that applies to a given issue or dispute. They learn how to do good legal research, and they can look forward to a career in which much of their time is spent in unheralded back room keypunching, far more than was expended by previous generations of lawyers who conducted legal research surrounded by three-foot high stacks of musty tomes.

The tendency to spend more time on legal research is accentuated by the fact that fewer cases get tried. Since law graduates are far more adept at researching the law than at trying cases, they emphasize their strong suit in representing a client, searching almost endlessly for the elusive perfect decision that will, they hope, persuade the opposition to settle, or the judge to favor their side in a pre-trial motion or in trial. An inexperienced lawyer commonly goes to extraordinary lengths to find alternatives to submitting a case to a jury, leading to an overkill in legal research and other pre-trial maneuvers. Meanwhile, the billable hour meter is running at the client's expense.

The desire of judges to avoid time-consuming trials can also, paradoxically, actually add to their workload, as well as to that of lawyers. Lawyers play to the judges' proclivity by filing long pre-trial motions, presenting the fruits of their legal research in the form of legal briefs submitted to the court. Each side seeks advantage in this manner by asking the judge to rule in its favor on various legal issues without a trial, since the jury can decide the facts, but the judge is supposed to decide the law. If, for example, the defense lawyer has located a case holding that skateboarding on public streets is illegal, the judge may be persuaded either to throw out the case or to make rulings that will favor one side, which also improves that side's position in any settlement negotiations.

Taken together, the modern ways lawsuits are handled have a profound impact on the working life of the lawyer. Far more time is consumed slogging through turgid documents and arid legal statutes, meticulously preparing to depose witnesses, and reviewing and analyzing legal cases than in giving ringing perorations to a jury. The exciting moments are fewer and farther apart. Seldom do the troops leave the trenches for hand-to-hand combat.

Clients are routinely dumbfounded to discover that their trial lawyer is almost never in court. The reality is that most of the trial lawyer's work is done in the office. On any given day, rather than soaring in the flight of oratorical wit, the lawyer's skills are more likely to be dedicated to painstakingly crafting cleverly worded answers to tortuous written interrogatories.

As I encountered these changes in the practice of law, I found myself marking my victories in smaller and smaller increments. Gaining a needed continuance, winning a minor discovery motion, unearthing a document helpful to my client's position—increasingly, such modest milestones of progress towards the inevitable settlement of a case became the highlights of a normal month of work. By shifting the measures of satisfaction, I attempted to convince myself that the practice of law remained an exciting profession. The truth is it has never been more boring to be a lawyer.

Successful lawyers today know that victory usually goes not to the valorous, but to those who dig the deepest and most meticulous trenches. To the plodding and persevering go the spoils.

# CHAPTER FIVE

# *A Lawyer's Dual Life*

From the very outset of my legal career, without realizing I was doing so, I searched for a set of uniform principles that would guide my behavior. Seeking to harmonize my personal and professional lives, I strove for a personal code that would govern both in my law practice and in my roles as husband, father, and friend. If I had taken the trouble to write them down, my basic personal/professional rules would have been along the lines of:

Be fair.

Be decent.

Be honest.

As a lawyer, I felt I had, by and large, succeeded in establishing a reputation for practicing within these principles. I was known as an effective but civil adversary. I was not one of those lawyers who needed to demonize the opposing lawyer in every hard-fought lawsuit. Many of my best friends in the bar were lawyers I had come to know as adverse counsel, sometimes in litigation that, from the client's perspective at least, was extremely acrimonious.

My efforts to apply the rules that succeeded so well in law practice to my personal life, however, especially to my marriage, met with diminished success over time. While I thought of myself as being a fair, decent, and honest husband, it became obvious that what was working at work wasn't working at home. I knew I was being much the same person in both contexts, and the simultaneous ascendancy of my professional career and decline of my marriage was profoundly puzzling to me. Every working day I was lauded and rewarded for the same behaviors that seemed to sink my marriage further into the morass. A succession of marriage counselors only highlighted the issues widening the gulf between my wife and me: lack of trust, a relationship that was more in synch rationally than emotionally, and difficulty in communicating.

As my marriage was failing, there was a period in which I supplemented counseling by devouring self-help books. Since each writer approached relationship problems differently, I thought the next book might contain the perfect key for me, for our relationship. During this period, I acquired one of the larger self-help libraries in the Western World. I immersed myself in the lingo of interpersonal sharing, caring, trusting, and communication. I haltingly began to put the pieces together, more from the totality of ideas than from any one perfect relationship guru.

Slowly at first, and then in a veritable gullywasher of revelations, certain new truths hit me like a ton of law books. My effort to lead my personal and professional lives by common principles was completely wrong. The twin halves of my life began to take differing shapes. It became clearer and clearer that the best self-help writers' prescriptions for healthy relationships derived from rules that would lead to disaster if applied in a law practice.

Honesty, for example, means something entirely different to marriage counselors than to lawyers. To a lawyer representing a client, honesty means the absence of fraud or perjury. To a skillful advocate, the description of a client's case consists of series of truthful statements that artfully marshal the facts most favorable to the client's perspective, while glossing over, explaining away, or omitting those facts that disfavor the client. Unless it happens to be prudent as a tactic, the trial lawyer or negotiator will not bare the weaknesses of the client, but will leave it to the adversary to discover and emphasize those weak points. Meanwhile, the other side's shortcomings are amplified and exaggerated.

Exaggeration of one's spouse's weaknesses is a sure-fire prescription for divorce. Honest communication within a marriage requires frequent and candid disclosure of one's own weaknesses, and the telling of half-truths is as dishonest and destructive as outright lying. An adversary presentation by the most ethical lawyer, when analyzed in the parlance of personal relationship psychology, would be taken, at best, as a collection of half-truths, if not utter falsehoods. The mere absence of fraud or perjury in personal communications reveals almost nothing about the truthfulness of the relationship. In short, pretty much any attempt to live by the lawyer's definition of honesty in a marriage will be woefully self-defeating.

Conversely, to conduct a legal practice in conformance with the recommended behaviors of self-help books would be calamitous. Just visualize your favorite touchy-feely caring person in the role of trial lawyer in a truculent lawsuit. Mr. Rogers may be wonderful in the neighborhood, but you'd never entrust your legal brief to him if you were in trouble.

I finally realized I needed two sets of optimal behaviors, one within a law practice and the other within a close relationship, both of which cannot be brought under the same principled umbrella. In fact, they are diametrically opposed. My long-term efforts to find common harmonizing rules of behavior for my work and my personal life were doomed to fail. I would have been better off assuming at the outset, as I concluded in the end, that conduct leading to a healthy law practice produces a sick marriage, and vice versa. While I remain convinced that one can achieve both a happy personal life and successful law practice, I have forever abandoned the notion that one unified set of rules or behaviors can lead to that result. A good lawyer, to be a good person, must learn to lead a dual life.

The subject of trust offers a pivotal example of the dual lives lawyers must lead. Has there ever been a self-help book or lecture that did not emphasize the centrality of trusting one another in personal relationships? The essence of the marital commitment is a leap of trust, the kind that presumes the best in a partner and holds to a conviction that trusting behaviors will be reciprocated in that relationship.

The cornerstone stance for a successful lawyer, especially a trial lawyer, is distrust. The best lawyers are instinctively distrustful, skeptically weighing each contention or statement made by the other side.

Take the example of a skillful insurance defense lawyer in action. When presented with a claim by a person injured in a car accident, the personal injury defense lawyer methodically sifts through the facts and file, and with an unspoken cynicism reviews each statement made by the claimant in a search for telltale signs of deceit. Was the light really green, as the plaintiff says? Was the plaintiff really well-rested and sober? Was the plaintiff's back injury caused solely by this accident, or was it more likely the recurrence of an injury suffered in high school football days? Are the plaintiff's claims that he is unable to work any more as a traveling salesman because driving aggravates his bad back consistent with other activities he is doing, such as waterskiing or shoveling snow? Such questions, asked endlessly, often hinge on the issue of trust. Since the assessment of this claim rests in large part upon the assertions made by the plaintiff, how much can he or she be trusted—or distrusted? It may be true that the claims are mostly truthful, but the best defense lawyers will zero in on the weakest links of the credibility chain as accurately as a laser-guided bomb.

To some extent, on an intellectual level at least, law schools teach the need to make this skeptical assessment of the other side's position. Students are taught to probe, to analyze, to make no unwarranted assumptions. Attention is given to detail, to logic, and to the need to dissect every claim critically.

But one's basic attitudes towards trusting are normally formed long before entering law school. A child raised in a family where one or both parents are deceitful about significant events and behaviors will have an ingrained understanding that basically good people sometimes lie, even to those they love. Just as important, he or she will gain a working knowledge of the nature of deceitful conduct, including the reality that the liar will often—indeed normally—cling tenaciously to the lie, even in the face of overwhelming evidence that contradicts it.

Consider, for example, the virtually universal experiences of those raised in a family affected by alcoholism. Every alcoholic is deceitful at times about drinking or about its impacts, and the family is usually positioned to both suffer from and learn by observing that deceit. A child who grows up hearing an alcoholic parent deny the reality of what everyone close to him or her is seeing cannot help but develop a more skeptical, distrustful attitude towards people. The child knows viscerally, without needing to be taught in law school or elsewhere, that even adamantly expressed claims made by people are sometimes totally false. Such a child has a head start on becoming a good lawyer, and has a better chance to excel in a profession that rewards distrusting instincts and behavior.

For those raised in healthier families, and to the extent family interaction was healthy, law school will be more difficult and law practice more challenging. To some degree, they will need to discard the presumptions of trust they acquired as children, and they will be left wondering why lawyers whose behaviors seem warped in a personal context often excel in practice. Where do these disturbing observations lead?

LESSON FIVE: *Aspiring lawyers raised in psychologically healthy families face more obstacles in law school and their careers than those raised in dysfunctional families. Personal traits learned in healthy families, such as honesty, sharing, open communication, and trusting, are dysfunctional in the practice of law. Over time and with much practice, psychologically healthy people can learn new skills to offset their personal traits, so they can achieve a successful legal career.*

Honesty and trusting are only two of many traits for which the imperatives of personal and professional behaviors diverge. Secret-keeping, manipulating other people, taking advantage of others' weaknesses, and rationalization—these behaviors also call for a dual approach if a lawyers hopes to be successful in both the professional and personal areas of his or her life. Illustrative cases are painfully clear and prevalent.

In a healthy family, secrets are most often fun, not hurtful. The whole idea behind wrapping a birthday present is to preserve a pleasurable secret. Guessing games are enhanced by the suspense created when one or more people know the secret and the other players fumble to discover it.

But in the dysfunctional family, secrecy assumes a sinister form. Children are routinely conscripted to keep the family's deepest, most painful secrets, whether they pertain to mental illness, drug dependency, incest, or any number of other disturbing forms of conduct. Such sick secrets are most fervently kept not just from strangers or casual acquaintances, but from other loved ones. Even close friends cannot be told that Daddy snorts cocaine. Aunt Tilda is the last one who should learn that Mom pops Valium like vitamins. And the secret that Mom's black eye came from Dad's fist rather than the stairway railing can never, never be told to Grandma.

Children in such families learn early how to keep secrets, especially important secrets withheld from those who would most like to know them, the secrets that are the most painful to keep. The keeping of secrets is part of the family pathology. Children raised in this environment become highly adept at secret-keeping, especially when emotions and stress are at their peaks. They commonly observe an adult keeping hurtful secrets with a completely straight face, often with an overlay of lies or half-truths. In these families, concealment of the truth is normal.

In the practice of law, secret-keeping is *de rigueur*. Lawyers are required to keep client confidences secret, no matter how hurtful the consequences to other people. A guilty rapist who confesses his guilt only to his lawyer will be set free to rape again unless there is sufficient evidence to convict him. The very best lawyer is one who, in the face of such knowledge, can exude confidence, even self-righteous indignation, that criminal charges have been brought against the client on such flimsy evidence. The lawyer will show no hint, by word, inflection, or facial expression, of the painful truth he or she knows. Most of the truly outstanding lawyers learned how to keep hurtful secrets long before entering law school, and their trial practice is a socially approved and highly rewarded outlet for a behavior that was destructive in their family.

As a day-to-day practice, the keeping of secrets in lawyering is not some pristine principle of non-disclosure. A raw emotional edge often accompanies the lawyer's secret-keeping, for the secret is as often kept for the purpose of doing damage to another as for protecting the client. Good lawyers erect elaborate strategies to shield the most damning truths from the other side. Poker-faced lawyers, skillfully employing half-truths, seek to divert the lawsuit from the discovery of the very evidence that would be most helpful to the opponent. In negotiations, a lawyer will lead the other side to believe that unimportant concessions are crucial, that essential conditions are routine. In trial, the cross-examining lawyer will reserve the nastiest surprises from his or her bag of tricks for the witness whose testimony, while truthful, is most helpful to the other side.

In each instance, the lawyer's actions are backed up by a secret. One who learned at an early age to keep important secrets has a huge advantage. In fact, I believe there is a serious question whether the lawyer's all-important skill of keeping hurtful secrets with emotional virtuosity can even be taught after childhood. The notion that confidences cannot be revealed can be learned, but no professor or text can teach the ability to convey, by gesture, body language and facial expression, a position that the lawyer knows to be false. Skills with an emotional essence are, for better or worse, taught most effectively at an early age.

Another skill invaluable in a law practice is the ability to manipulate people. Everyone comes into a lawsuit, as he or she goes through life, blessed with some personal strengths and burdened with human frailties. Since the evidence in trials is presented mainly through the testimony of people, good lawyering depends in large part on the careful use and adroit abuse of witnesses.

One of the keys to success in trial is creating the circumstances which use a witness's weaknesses to the benefit of the advocate's cause. Witnesses who are stubborn or obstinate can often be made to appear as though they are withholding crucial evidence, even when the lawyer knows they are not. Witnesses with a shiftless or guiltily nervous demeanor can be made out to be liars when they are not. Witnesses with pent up hostility can be made to appear more violent than they are in actuality. There is a frightful rush of exhilaration that comes with having the skill, the virtually certain ability, to choreograph a series of questions, exhibits, and other evidence in a fashion that advances the client's cause by destroying a crucial opposing witness through dexterous manipulation of his or her weaknesses.

I once interviewed an alibi witness in a multiple murder case, a timid man who was a walking catalogue of shifty behaviors. He had a habit of pausing before answering each question, during which time he blinked repeatedly and then stared upwards as though the answer was written in the ceiling tiles. His answers to the simplest questions came with such muttering and hesitation that he appeared to be making them up even when I was covering a topic where I knew he was telling the truth. While he was ultimately never called at any trial, I will never forget the surge of professional power I felt when I realized that this witness could be made to seem to be lying about any subject. If I handled him properly, no one would ever believe him. To this day, I don't know whether his alibi testimony was truthful, but I do know that I could have convinced any jury that it was not.

Children raised in dysfunctional families are likely to receive an extensive education in manipulative behaviors long before law school. They will observe, usually repeatedly and graphically, the minuets of manipulation in their parents' and relatives' unhealthy relationships. The physically abusive husband, for example, may manipulate the wife's lack of self-esteem to the point that she accepts blame for her own beatings. The same wife may manipulate her remorseful husband to gain ends she otherwise could not achieve. The pattern of mutual manipulation repeats itself, teaching the child about the very dynamic of manipulation itself. The lesson that one's own purposes can be served by maneuvering another person into a position that takes advantage of his or her personal weaknesses, combined with the realization that most people cling even to utterly destructive personality traits in times of stress, is tremendously helpful in the practice of law.

In a classic good news/bad news fashion, growing up in a manipulative family simply makes a lawyer feel more comfortable with one of his or her necessary roles. Manipulation of others arouses greater discomfort in those unaccustomed to living with it. What was pathological in the family is welcomed, even essential, in the practice of law. Here, too, those who grew up in non-manipulative environments will have some catching up to do as lawyers.

Rationalization is yet another indispensable legal skill learned at the parental knees. Rationalizing consists of devising convincing but incorrect reasons for events or behaviors. The reasons may be technically true but fundamentally false, such as when the alcoholic with a hangover says he's late for work because he's "not feeling well," or when the wife who has spent a sleepless night in heated argument with her husband says, "I look tired because I just couldn't get to sleep last night." These statements are correct, but not really true.

Life in a dysfunctional family is an endless series of rationalizations:

- "If you didn't make me so angry, I wouldn't beat you."
- "I drink because my life is so hard."
- "I'm sure he'll stop snorting cocaine when he lands a job."

When statements like these fill the air at home, people raised in such an atmosphere become highly proficient at thinking up untrue, or hypertechnically true, reasons for what they do, and for what goes on around them. After years of family conditioning, the line between truth and rationalized truth becomes indistinguishable, enabling the person raised in this environment to speak with great conviction in support of a statement that would plague the conscience of someone brought up in a healthy family.

The ability to rationalize quickly and convincingly is an essential skill of lawyering. Whatever charge of wrongdoing is hurled against the client, the lawyer who can compile a list of innocent reasons for the client's behavior has a leg up in the adversary process. "The accident occurred not because my client was speeding recklessly in a residential zone, but because a freak and sudden rainstorm caused him to lose control on a slick surface." "My client lied to the police about the crime not because he was dishonest, but because he was scared." "We are seeking a long delay in the trial of this case not to hinder or to wear down our opposition, Your Honor, but because we need lots of time to investigate these complicated facts." The list goes on and on. The reasons given are not false. The road really was wet, the client was scared, and the case is complicated. But frequently the proffered facts are only a convenient peg upon which to hang a type of deception. I'm not talking about dishonest lawyers here, but about conscientious lawyers who are routinely presenting the facts in a light most favorable to their client's purposes.

Those who master the art of rationalization at an early age by aping their parents will be at an advantage in the practice of law. All others will need remedial tutoring before they can achieve greatness at the bar.

Although extreme personal dysfunctions call for a complex analysis that is beyond my level of expertise, two deviant psychological traits—paranoia and hostility—can be more functional in the profession than we lawyers would like to admit. True paranoia is a serious psychotic state in which the sufferer erects elaborately reasoned explanations for delusional persecution. It does not stretch the imagination greatly, however, to see how a person infused with streaks of paranoia can be a particularly effective and convincing trial lawyer. Who could better marshal the facts to show that the prosecution is a conspiracy to convict the client than a paranoiac? Who could better pore through masses of evidence and become totally certain that the other side is motivated to persecute the client?

One Bible-thumping disbarred lawyer with whom I dealt comes to mind here. Convinced that the federal reserve system was at the root of all the country's ills, he argued that U.S. money was unconstitutional and should not be accepted as legal tender. He had a spell-binding ability to make absurd propositions sound plausible, in part because he could embrace even crazy ideas with total conviction. I was told that he had been a mesmerizing jury lawyer in the days before his disbarment, and, even seeing him in the days after his connection with the real world had slipped, I had no doubt of it. The line between a controlled and positively channeled form of paranoia and a psychotic state may be narrower than is comfortable to acknowledge.

Hostility, psychologically speaking, is extreme and unwarranted anger. People with hostile behaviors have a hair trigger for rageful conduct. When provoked even slightly, they act a bit like Dobermans or pit bulls. They have personality traits that, particularly when masked by a veneer of rationality or outward calm, are actively sought by many vengeful clients. Their lashing verbal diatribes can literally evoke the same sense of fear as bared fangs. And their behavior is most effective when it is completely in character, when everyone knows or soon learns that they are born (or raised) snarlers. Law professors haven't a clue as to how to teach this behavior, and most have absolutely no wish to do so. Such skills are either ingrained or can be learned only at home.

One of the most odious people I have ever met was a lawyer who had the ability to ooze reason and charm before the court or jury one minute, and then a minute later in the court house corridor during a recess, purple-faced and spitting vituperation, hurl vile obscenities and personal insults at the opposing lawyer. In almost every case, he attempted to rattle the opposition with similarly rageful behavior out of court. He was also in tremendous demand as a trial lawyer.

COROLLARY TO LESSON FIVE: *You don't have to be screwed up to be a good lawyer, but it may help.*

# CHAPTER SIX

## *The Joke's on Us*

Q. What do you call 10,000 lawyers at the bottom of the sea?
A. A good start.

&ast; &ast; &ast;

Q. What do a lawyer and a sperm cell have in common?
A. Each has a one-in-a-million chance of becoming a human being.

&ast; &ast; &ast;

Q. What's the difference between a dead skunk and a dead lawyer on the highway?
A. There are skid marks in front of the skunk.

&ast; &ast; &ast;

Q. Why does California have the most lawyers and New Jersey the most toxic-waste dumps?
A. New Jersey got first choice.

&ast; &ast; &ast;

A Rabbi, a Hindu priest, and a lawyer were traveling together in the countryside and needed a place to stay late at night. They stumbled onto a farmhouse and asked the farmer if he could put them up. The farmer said he would be glad to accommodate them, but that he only had room for two in the house; one person would have to sleep in the barn.

The Hindu priest volunteered first to sleep in the barn, only to return in a few minutes, saying, "There is a cow in the barn, and my religion forbids me to sleep with cows."

The Rabbi volunteered next, but he also came back to the house soon, saying, "There is a pig in the barn, and my religion forbids me to sleep with pigs."

Finally, the lawyer offered to sleep in the barn. A few minutes later, there was a knock at the farmhouse door.

It was the pig.

Lawyer jokes are not a new phenomenon. What is new is their venomous tone. For many years, the punch line of lawyer jokes typically hinged on lawyers' exorbitant fees or endemic dishonesty. Recently, though, the jokes have turned on the notion that lawyers are the scum of the earth, often implying that their elimination would bring the betterment of all: the only good lawyer is a dead lawyer. At a time when even bland ethnic jokes are deemed offensive and unfairly stereotyping, no crudity is too great and no crack too vile for lawyer jokes.

Why are lawyers the object of such vitriolic scorn? To some extent, of course, it has always been so. Shakespeare's oft-quoted line—"The first thing we do, let's kill all the lawyers"—evidences the timeless appeal of morbid humor directed at lawyers. The current spate of lawyer jokes might be seen as merely a periodic revival of an ageless target of ridicule.

But I fear that lawyer jokes today illuminate more somber issues. To understand why jokes that utterly vilify an entire profession are so heatedly embraced, it is worthwhile to consider what lawyers are doing that might evoke this response.

As they themselves would point out, lawyers often stand at the pivotal juncture between our democratic polity and its sometimes perverse will. We often forget that our Constitution's Bill of Rights is not merely an abstract collection of personal rights, but an unequivocal declaration that such rights are to be maintained sacrosanct even against the strong desires of the majority of the people.

The very acts of the government—our democratically elected government—are circumscribed by the Bill of Rights. Congress itself is prohibited from making any law that:

      -abridges free speech,

      -interferes with freedom of religious expression,

      -denies the right to due process in court.

It matters not whether the overwhelming popular consensus at any given time favors a partial or temporary suspension of certain personal rights. The Constitution is designed to prevent us from achieving these democratic wishes, most especially when the many wish to run roughshod over the rights of a few.

On each occasion when a law is passed that arguably infringes on Constitutional rights, even rights most find unpalatable, lawyers are seen to stand up for those who resist the majority's will. The Nazi, the Communist, the politically incorrect of whatever stripe all have the assistance of legal counsel whose very presence tweaks those of us who might sympathize with the majority. When the principle of free religious expression is challenged, a lawyer will come forth not only in its defense, but also to profess the freedom of religious cults to brainwash converts. Wherever there is an outspoken boor or wretched distributor of political hate literature, there is usually a lawyer not far behind to argue for his or her rights. That lawyer's argument is most often a claim that you—you who hold the reins of power and comprise the prevailing viewpoint in this free and democratic society—have trampled on the rights of the client.

It is no wonder that lawyers enter the professional popularity tournament with a substantial handicap. Wherever the democratic majority seeks to go, a lawyer pops up wagging his or her adversarial finger in our faces. Lawyers are perennially associated with every person or cause we dislike. The taint of advocacy for abhorred causes cannot help but rub off on lawyers.

But lawyers' role in the preservation of unpopular rights hardly explains the especially nasty turn taken by lawyer jokes in the '90's. After all, lawyers have advocated rights for the disfavored since the Constitution was adopted.

The rising wave of crime, particularly violent crime, affords another possible explanation for this recent phenomenon. As we grow more fearful of and angry at those who rip apart our sense of personal safety, as crime itself seems to spread like an unchecked malignancy, the temptation is great to blame lawyers, at least in part. The more heinous and widespread criminal acts are in a society, the more opportunities the public has to witness lawyers in league with criminals. The rapist who chopped off his victim's hands had a lawyer, as did the California serial murder night stalker. Every criminal condemned to death by judge or jury has legal counsel, sometimes a phalanx of lawyers. It is plausible to surmise that a sudden drop in the incidence of violent crime in America would be accompanied by a rise in the ranking of lawyers in popularity polls.

Nevertheless, I doubt that higher crime statistics account for much of the contemporary scorn for lawyers. We have always had villainous criminals, and they have always been defended by lawyers, some of whom became legendary doing so. The frightening increase in the crime rate makes lawyers look worse only by a matter of degree.

Pondering the unpopularity of lawyers, I am always reminded of my experiences in the early 1970's as a divorce lawyer, and of the contrast between my divorce clients and my other cases. It almost goes without saying that divorce clients dislike their spouses' lawyers. At a time of ultimate personal vulnerability, the other lawyer is often viewed as an unadulterated oppressor, willing to use guile and legal tricks to take advantage of a person in turmoil.

A more interesting phenomenon is divorce clients' reactions to their own lawyers. Through experience, I learned to apply two rules to domestic relations cases: (1) never represent a good business client in a divorce, and (2) never forget that Jesus Christ himself would have been hated by some of his clients had he been a divorce lawyer.

The reason for both rules was the same: the divorcing process is so uniquely painful, so inherently acrimonious, and so emotionally upsetting that some clients cannot help but detest anyone identified with that slice of themselves or that part of their life. During a divorce, otherwise decent people do ghastly things to people they have loved. Children and property cannot be divided without emotional anguish. No legal apportionment of the pieces of shattered dreams seems fair to the parties to a divorce.

Whenever I represented a business client in a divorce, the chances were good he or she would never want to see me again after the divorce was over, no matter what the result. So I routinely referred him or her to another divorce lawyer.

I came to accept the fact that a certain proportion of my divorce clients would forever viscerally recoil at my very presence. While they would have given a series of rational explanations for their aversion to me, such as the high fees charged, excessive delays, or grumbles about sundry bad advice, the actual basis for their feelings usually was that I had come to symbolize the most wretched experience of their lives. On a deeper level, however, I sensed that their feelings for me were inextricably tied to an intense, if unacknowledged, pocket of self-loathing they wanted to seal shut forever.

It is human nature to abhor those who remind us of our gravest flaws. And it is the experience of divorce lawyers, writ large on the face of society as a whole that, I believe, best explains Americans' wholesale disregard for lawyers today.

Lawyers serve as constant reminders of some our most grievous shortcomings as individuals and as a nation. It's little wonder we tell jokes likening them to pond scum. While some lawyers deserve the comparison, the ugly turn in lawyer jokes is more a reflection of a mass feeling of self-revulsion towards certain trends in our society than a reaction to any changes in lawyers' behavior or even to lawyers themselves. When we direct gallows humor at lawyers, it is in apprehension that the hangman lurks uncomfortably close to all of us. The lesson here extends far beyond mere joke telling.

LESSON SIX: *The greater the public demand for legal remedies and services, the greater the public's scorn of lawyers.*

Americans cling to the myth that we are a nation of rugged individualists. What's wrong is wrong, what's right is right, and we don't need government, laws, or lawyers to tell us which is which. Our cherished myths take us back to the days when a handshake, rather than a pack of lawyers, sealed a deal. Bring back the times when ordinary folks elected to public office wrote the laws, before the lawyers controlled it all, people say. Give us the swift, if rough, justice meted out on the frontier, rather than the hidebound procedures and delays of today's overly protective courts.

It is widely believed that lawyers write the new laws that take us as a nation farther from the ideal of rugged individualism, and that they do so as much to feather their own nests as to serve any public purpose. Lawyers, and no one else, the modern mythology goes, benefit from the plethora of laws that afflicts us all.

The truth is that, although Americans respond to the rhetoric of individual ruggedness, they vote with an ever more legalistic fervor. Especially since the 1960's, this lawyer-hating nation of individualists has supported—demanded, even—measure after measure enacting new rights that can be enforced only through lawyers and courts. This unprecedented adoption of new legal rights and remedies has been accomplished through our elected legislatures that, at the state level at least, have far fewer lawyer members than they did thirty years ago.

The clamor for legal solutions to social problems comes most resoundingly from ordinary citizens, not lawyers. The notion that lawyers have procured this outcome against the public will overlooks the fact that lawyers, however much their ranks may have been swelled and however influential they may be, still account for far less than one percent of the population.

America does have more lawyers per capita than any other country in the world, but our ascendancy to that dubious distinction did not come by straight line growth. During the more than 100-year period from the Civil War to 1970, the number of lawyers in America merely kept pace with the population expansion. The number of lawyers was proportionately the same when Lincoln was assassinated as when Kennedy was.

But from 1970 to 1990, the growth in the percentage of lawyers far outstripped population increases for the first time in our history. During those twenty years, the size of the legal profession grew at twice the population rate. We now have more than 800,000 American lawyers, up from 200,000 in 1970. By the turn of the century, we are expected to surpass the one million mark. If we project this pattern of increase into the future, we will have more lawyers than teachers and doctors combined by about the year 2040, and by the year 2095 there will be more lawyers than people.

The current glut of lawyers is well publicized. Nonetheless, law schools continue to be besieged with far more applicants than they have vacancies. Human resources keep flowing into the legal profession. Many of the best and brightest students who in earlier times would have become teachers, preachers, or business leaders have flocked to the law. In this generation, law has effectively siphoned extraordinary personal talent from almost every other important sector of our society.

But the continuing demand for a legal education, which is driven by the often incorrect perceptions of today's undergraduates, does not explain the huge rise in the demand for legal services. The notion that more lawyers beget more law and create more legal services is true only to a point.

When I started practicing, many of the small towns in Minnesota had only a single lawyer. Keeping pace with the growth in lawyering elsewhere, most of those same towns now have several lawyers. In the '70's, the old saw used to be: "If there's only one lawyer in town, he or she drives a Buick. If there are two, they both drive Cadillacs." There is an element of truth in the idea that two or more lawyers foment disputes whereas one lawyer would work out disagreements among existing clients. But today's sequel to the old saw is that now there are six lawyers in town, and they all drive Pintos.

The biggest single explanation for the geometric increase in the number of lawyers is not that they are all whipping up more legal work, but rather our society's splashy plunge into the regulation of conduct previously left to individual discretion. Wrongs that have been around for millennia are now expected to be righted by laws, lawsuits, and courts. The very essence of the concept of rugged individualism, an ability to take the brunt of life's blows and misfortunes upon oneself, settle one's own scores, and persevere despite it all, is no longer embraced by the majority of Americans.

We have so transformed our basic outlook that it is no longer even acceptable, let alone sanctified, to confront life's countless adversities without suing those whom we perceive have wronged us. Instead of finding ways around obstacles, we have been led to believe—and most of us now do believe—that we must act aggressively to vindicate our rights. A person who fails to see a lawyer when wronged is no longer lauded but derided as an Uncle Tom, a weak sister, a wimp. Lawyers may prosper financially, but are denigrated collectively as a consequence.

The examples of our legal-centrism are so many as to be easily overlooked. As recently as 1970, child abuse, both sexual and physical, was largely a familial rather than legal issue. In the two decades since, we have embraced the praiseworthy notion that children have the right to be free from abuse, and our efforts to assure that right have led to employment for thousands of social workers and lawyers.

In an effort to create safer workplaces, OSHA and other laws have been enacted, again swelling the ranks of the bureaucracy and the legal profession. Politically popular environmental protection laws now regulate everything from land use to waste disposal—and afford employment to lawyers. Consumer protection laws ranging from truth-in-lending to product safety to food and drug standards have multiplied, all requiring legal interpretation and establishing new grounds for lawsuits.

Civil rights laws enacted with passionate mandates and dedicated to the most noble objectives have spawned a thicket of rules, agencies, and court decisions that reach every corner of the economy and human relations. What started with the goal of opening public lunch counters and the front of the bus to all races now touches every employment application form and every office personnel manual. The by-product of this laudable effort to reduce the impact of prejudice has been, out of necessity, a direct increase in the number of lawyers to decipher rules, represent litigants, and staff government agencies.

What is more, civil rights laws continue to serve as our blueprint for ameliorating many other social problems. Legislation and litigation, rather than leadership or moral suasion, are the ready solutions we throw at every issue.

Nowhere is this development more apparent than in the rapidly expanding field of employment law. Hoards of unhappy employees are besieging the courts, sometimes with claims that rest upon no more than unspoken but fervently held assumptions that they have a right not to be fired, not to be passed over for promotion, not to be insulted, not to be slighted, or not to be adversely affected in any way in the workplace. With the aid of creative lawyers, those who cast themselves as victims dress up their perceptions in varying legal theories, most of which boil down to some kind of right not to be treated unfairly. So much for the rugged individual. So much for the idea of rebounding from the hard knocks of life, and forging ahead.

Wherever you look these days, some public official or crusading citizen is proposing to extend the frontiers of remedies under law. We are on the verge of embracing such propositions as: spanking is actionable child abuse; children dissatisfied with their parents can "divorce" them; a job, once obtained, is an entitlement, not a privilege; smoking anywhere outside your own home should be prohibited; and short, tall, fat, skinny, or ugly people are entitled to sue someone who fails to treat them like all others. We are now dedicated to the proposition that life's vicissitudes must be lessened or eliminated by law, that every conceivable inequity carries with it the compulsion to create a legal right to remedy the wrong.

More fundamentally, as the traditional barriers against use of legalistic solutions have peeled away, virtually everyone turns to the law more readily. Even business people, who decry the growth of lawyers generally, have become far more likely to resort to legalistic answers. If cash flow is bad or problems arise in a business deal, the knee-jerk response is to see a lawyer. Find out your rights. Sue if it might serve a business purpose. In business, the idea that a lawsuit is a last-ditch solution no longer prevails.

During the past thirty years, American society has altered itself from being determined to overcome obstacles to being fixated upon hammering away at the obstacles themselves. Patients whose doctors are the best-trained in the world routinely second-guess treatment given. They expect a cure for every ailment and increasingly see a lawyer when it's not forthcoming. Whoever even dreamed of suing teachers or school administrators thirty years ago? Now almost every school district needs a trial lawyer to deal with claims by disgruntled parents and citizens. Time after time, the answers to problems are the same: See a lawyer. Pass a law. Sue. Stand up for your rights. It is no coincidence that the explosive growth of the legal profession has exactly paralleled these changes in our society.

Although all societies need dispute resolution systems, we stand alone in the extent to which we insist that law and courts are the answer to the problems every society faces. Many people go though life today defining every setback as an injustice, and we Americans have demanded a legal system that spoon-feeds this proclivity. The result is a kind of misfortune-driven symbiosis. Democratically adopted rights and remedies engorge the legal profession, and legalistic avenues become the solution of choice for all difficulties.

But this devotion of more and more resources to the redress of wrongs has the unintended effect of undermining, at least in part, our capacity to build what's right. Lawsuits inevitably amplify the negative facets of life and are inherently backward looking. By focusing on his or her grievances, often for months or even years of legal proceedings, a person can be diverted from facing or planning for the future. The same focus writ large throughout a nation is highly disturbing.

From my experience, a client's perception of the personal victimization he or she has endured is almost always greater than the reality. Every time a court decision, law, or regulation trumpets the establishment of a new right, some benefits flow to those legitimately wronged, but malcontents also have another weapon at their disposal. Instead of chiding or even ostracizing those whose behavior is litigious or complaining, we lionize those who bring lawsuits as crusaders, place them on pillars for standing up for their rights, and for the rights of others. As long as it is gussied up in legalisms, it has never been more socially acceptable to be a jerk.

The frontiers of legally defined injustice, constantly expanding as they are, represent the modern equivalent of the doctrine of Manifest Destiny. America is as devoted today to pushing back the borders of wrongdoing as it was dedicated in the last century to filling the geography between the Atlantic and Pacific Oceans.

Yet, just as my divorce clients did, somewhere deep down we Americans loathe ourselves for our own behavior. We hate our sniveling aversion to risk, our governmental intrusions into the confines of the family, our burgeoning bureaucracies essential to safeguard the newly created protections we demand, and our penchant for tilting a legal lance at every nefarious windmill.

We despise lawyers because they personify a society run amuck with rights consciousness, with an excess of government, and with a contentious and fundamentally negative view of the world. We tell jokes wishing all lawyers were dead while we pass yet more laws and praise court decisions giving birth to more of them.

# CHAPTER SEVEN

# *The Almighty Billable Hour*

Almost thirty years have elapsed since I last punched a time clock as a day laborer in my family's floral and gardening store. Yet I distinctly recall the vertical cardboard card with pre-printed lines given me every two weeks to log my work time. When inserted into the slot in the center of the time clock, the manila card was imprinted with the exact minute of my arrival or departure. The imprint was accompanied by a metallic ring that was duller than a cash register but resounded with more force and authority. As the two-week pay period progressed, the lines on the card became filled with the entries proving my labors, which were then converted arithmetically into a paycheck. At the end of a summer of work, I derived some measure of personal self-worth merely from the knowledge that I had created a stack of cards as tangible evidence.

A lawyer's time sheets, or time records, are far more detailed than my old time cards, which simply recorded the
hours of my physical presence at the workplace. For every
day I was engaged in the private practice of law, I recorded
my time in 15-minute increments. Just as a gosling is imprinted to follow the first larger creature it encounters in
life as its parent, even if that creature happens to be the
barnyard golden retriever, I attempted to maintain the rules
of logging time I first learned, resisting efforts in later years
to alter the mechanics or to computerize the process.

It is a mark of the indelible impression left by the first
stage of the endlessly repeated administrivia of life that I
have a clearer memory of the time sheets I used when I
began practice than of my oldest child's first words or early
birthday parties. Those first time sheets were green, with
pre-printed spaces to be filled in by hand indicating the
client's name, the services provided, and the time spent.

Literally thousands of times, I wrote:

-"ABC Corporation: Telephone conference with client re summary judgment motion—15 minutes," or

-"Lincoln Jones: Legal research re statute of limitations—45 minutes," or

-"Universal Plastics, Inc.: Travel to and from courthouse and appearance before Judge Swanson on defendant's
motion to compel discovery—two hours and 15 minutes."

At the end of each day, I gave these entries to my secre-
tary, who in earlier days manually typed them on client
billing sheets and in later days entered them into the law
firm's computerized billing records.

The details of tracking time vary from law firm to law
firm. Some firms record time by bits as small as one-tenth

of an hour, or even by the minute, whereas I was taught that any service worth the effort of recording the time deserved to be billed at a minimum of one-quarter of an hour. Some firms insist upon an elaborate description of the services provided, while some prefer unrevealing generalities like "legal services rendered." But these differences are all subsumed by the enshrined rule of modern American lawyering that a lawyer's worth is measured and a client is most often charged by a rate linked to the relentless tick of the clock: the billable hour.

It would be hard to overestimate the ascendant importance of billable hours in our legal profession. They are the litmus test of the worth and financial success of a lawyer or law firm. A lawyer who allows his or her annual billable hours to slip too low, or a firm that drops below the prevailing billable hour norms for its community, risks more than a decrease in income. Survival, of the lawyer within the firm or of the law firm itself, is at stake. Larger law firms exist today in an environment driven more by overall financial performance than by the quality of legal work generated or the reputation of its lawyers in the community. No one makes any meaningful effort to rank the quality of the lawyering done by these firms, but, for about the past ten years, national legal tabloids like *The National Law Journal* and similar local publications like *Minnesota's Journal of Law & Politics* have routinely published comparative rankings of law firms' financial performance. The surest way to move up or down in these rankings is to adjust the minimum number of billable hours expected of lawyers.

One fact predominates in any discussion of the role of billable hours over the past twenty years in American law practice: virtually every firm now requires its lawyers to bill substantially more hours than in the past. There has been a universal trend to increase the minimum floor of hours, the firm's "billable hours budget," for every lawyer, whether partner or associate. It is now standard for Wall Street firms to mandate minimum hours of 2,000 or more per year, and for other large firms around the country to require billings approaching that amount.

Twenty years ago, there was much less emphasis on the billable hour, and the time commitment to law practice leeway given to individual lawyers was far wider. Lawyers with average billings of 1,500 hours per year often became partners; the same time sheet performance today would be considered grossly substandard. Across the country, lawyers' lives have been transformed by a ceaseless spiral of mandated workaholism.

The reasons for the universal increase in law firm work hours can be viewed from two perspectives: that of the managing partners and that of the beginning associate. The managing partners of any firm are responsible for its business functioning, its financial performance, its profitability for partners. The way most law firms bill their clients—a stated hourly rate times hours billed—circumscribes management options. Since the costs of operation, including rent, secretarial salaries, computer equipment, and supplies, are relatively fixed, profits can only be increased by raising either billing rates or billable hours.

From a business point of view, raising the lawyers' hours budget is preferable to hiking rates because the change is invisible to clients. A firm that boosts the rate of the average partner from $190 to $200 per hour runs the risk of becoming less competitive in the local legal marketplace. Both current and potential future clients may take their legal work elsewhere to avoid the higher fees. Increasing the annual hours budget from 1,900 to 2,000 yields the same proportional rise in partners' profits, but without any detrimental effect upon competition between firms. Because costs are basically fixed, every extra hour worked and billed drops almost totally to the partners' bottom line.

But managing partners' financial woes extend far beyond a straightforward calculation of work hours times billing rates, due to another new development in the last generation—the "lateral" move of lawyers from firm to firm. In the 1960's, it was still considered improper for one law firm to hire a lawyer away from a competitive firm. Today, the hiring of laterals, both partners and associates, is one of the biggest sources of law firm growth. Every legal community is now constantly abuzz with gossip about the latest law firm defections and additions, and a firm's standing can fluctuate like the Dow Jones average depending on the latest moves. "Did you hear that Schwartz left Pickering last month to head the probate department at Trueblood? That makes three lost partners for Pickering in six months. If this keeps up, they're in real trouble."

While lawyers switch firms for many reasons, the lateral departures most dreaded by the managing partner are those involving the "most productive"—read "highest billing"—lawyers. To understand the inordinate financial impact of such a loss, consider a simplified hypothetical breakdown. If the average lawyer in a firm bills 1,800 hours per year, and the costs of operating the firm are about 50% of total proceeds, 900 hours of effort goes to pay overhead. A partner billing at the rate of $200 per hour will contribute $360,000 to the firm's proceeds, $180,000 of which will pay costs and the same amount will be distributable through the partnership "pie." But a partner who bills 2,400 hours will generate $480,000 in firm income for only slightly higher costs, say $200,000. The net return from the harder working partner would, in this example, be $280,000, or $100,000 more than the firm average. By working "only" 50% longer hours, the workaholic raises his or her contribution to partnership profits by about 65%. In other words, a partner's economic benefit to the firm is raised disproportionately by work habits that depart upwards from the firm's average.

Making calculations similar to this one, unhappy partners whose work habits are out of synch with others in their firm complain that their compensation is being dragged down. If entreaties to raise the firm's hourly budget are unsuccessful, or if the firm is unwilling to cut off a much larger slice of the compensation pie, the disaffected drone can jump laterally to another firm, typically one where the financial benefit of spreading the overhead among other like-minded time-grinders is maximized.

In this manner, the managing partners who permit their billable hours budgets to fall out of line with the local competition risk far more than a slight imbalance in partners' income. The partnership itself can recede through erosion of its size and, more importantly, loss of reputation, when lawyers jump laterally.

The other impetus for escalating work hours comes, ironically, from starting associates. Several years ago, when I was serving as a member of my law firm's management committee, I fielded numerous complaints from young lawyers about the pressures caused by the time demands of practice. Those with families were especially hard hit. Unlike the era when I began practice, when a (usually male) lawyer was seldom married to a working professional, by the 1980's most of our married young associates came from two-career homes. They almost uniformly urged me to hold the line on the billable hours budget and to resist boosting our hours requirements to match recent hikes by other large firms.

Responding to these pleas, I supported a recruitment approach that differed from our competitors'. Our firm decided to maintain its starting salary (then at $44,000, as I recall) and to emphasize that our billable hours budget was only 1,650 a year—at least 150 hours below that of firms that had increased their starting salaries to $50,000. We reasoned that the top law students would flock to a firm that offered a relatively high salary coupled with a more balanced and civilized lifestyle.

That year turned out to be the worst ever for our firm's recruitment efforts. Faced with crushing student loans of up to $75,000 to repay—and oblivious to the realities of the life they would face when billing 1,800 to 2,000 hours a year—candidates for associate positions opted in almost every instance for the higher salary instead of fewer work hours. By now, of course, these same students, as young lawyers, are expressing misgivings about their harried and overworked lives. If only they had known as law students what they now know, my guess is most of them would gladly have sacrificed incremental dollars for a more balanced life.

From hard-earned experience, I have come up with a rough rule of thumb for those who contemplate some form of life outside the practice of law, a life involving, say, marriage, children, hobbies or outside interests.

LESSON SEVEN: *10% of a lawyer's soul dies for every 100 billable hours worked in excess of 1,500 per year.*

While one may quibble about the number or percentages, the conclusion that lawyering carried to excess is destructive to one's personal life is beyond reasonable dispute. The lawyer's professional life is filled with aggressive, manipulative, half-truthful and other destructive behaviors, most of which are necessary, if unfortunate, by-products of our adversary system. If one wishes to salvage a measure of humane existence from a life spent in the aggressive pursuit of other people's causes, one must keep billable hours below 1,500 a year.

At 1,500 hours, there is time not only to attend Johnny's school pageant, play the clarinet, go fishing, or join a study group at the synagogue, but also to find a sufficient respite from lawyering behaviors to offer a personal sanctuary or counterbalance.

Law students, who are accustomed to working long hours during law school, fail to appreciate the long-term significance of a lifetime regimen premised on 2,000 annual billable hours. Multiplying fifty weeks per year times forty hours, they conclude that 2,000 hours can be achieved by a work week less than the forty to fifty hours of their law school efforts. But that analysis ignores the difference between actual hours and billable hours, and also fails to comprehend the difference between the pressures of law school, which are basically intellectual, and the added strains that come with lawyerly responsibilities.

Young lawyers soon learn the distinction between hours spent working and billable hours. The truth is that one needs to work 55-60 hours to bill forty. For starters, ordinary daily activities and pleasantries, such as greetings and chit-chat with co-workers and secretaries, coffee breaks, and bathroom breaks cannot be billed. When I punched a manual laborer's time clock, I was given credit for such time.

Paid holidays and vacations assume a different meaning to someone whose efforts are measured by annual billable hours. Young lawyers' friends who are in other fields of work are surprised to learn that law firms do not specify holidays or the number of vacation days permitted. A starting associate may feel a kind of heady smugness when he or she says, "As long as I get my hours in, I can take as many holiday or vacation days as I want."

The reality is that it's harder to take a vacation from yourself than from an employer. A billable hour system means that the cell door is open but a massive ball and chain remain invisibly attached. Come November, the associate whose hours are below budget—whether due to a dearth of work, a death in the family, attendance at career-enhancing legal education courses, or virtually any other reason—will be more likely to rescind that planned December vacation than if Scrooge himself were setting the work rules. As for holidays one came to expect as a given in law school, one soon learns that law firms are open and practicing hard on the days other employers give over to commemorating the deeds of national heroes, such as Martin Luther King, Lincoln, Washington, and Columbus. For an associate, these national holidays simply mean that he or she must send legal documents by fax or Fed Ex, rather than by U.S. mail.

Law students are largely unaware that the fastest-growing chunk of time commitments for practicing lawyers is the law-related *non*-billable hour. Lawyers are expected to spend an ever-increasing amount of time on a wide variety of non-recompensable duties: on law firm committees that do everything from manage the firm to select the office artwork; on recruiting and interviewing job applicants; on bar association and other professional activities; on reviewing the newest cases or legal developments; on attending continuing legal education courses.

Another enormous time-gobbler for all lawyers is what is euphemistically referred to as "marketing," an area that has been dramatically altered during the past two decades. In 1970, the law firms with which I interviewed assured me that the days were gone when lawyers were hired for their business or social contacts. A listing in the social register or membership in the poshest country club was irrelevant. The common pitch was: "We get and keep clients solely because of the quality legal work we do and the reputation that flows from that work." In those days, beginning lawyers were told not to worry about, or spend time on, attracting new clients. At that time, when the demand for sophisticated legal services outstripped supply, this message was more than recruiting hype. It was true.

The transformation of the legal marketplace within the past twenty years has added to the work burdens of lawyers on a daily basis. From the outset, lawyers today are taught that attracting, obtaining, and keeping clients is required of everyone in the firm. The same large law firms that calmly assured the law students of the '60's and '70's that client-getting skills were completely unnecessary in their practice now inform even first-year associates that their marketing ability will be weighed heavily in considering admission to the partnership. Lawyers are expected to join clubs, give practicum seminars, write newsletters aimed at clients, and develop and follow up leads for new clients to an extent never before demanded. All of this time spent attracting and schmoozing clients translates to non-billable hours, which are simply added on top of the minimum work requirements of the firm.

Within the firm, a lawyer must be seen as causing the practice to grow, not merely improving his or her legal skills. A stunningly capable lawyer is less favored than a more mediocre marketing whiz. When I opted for law school over an MBA, I thought I was leaving the economically-driven hurly-burly of the business world for a dignified profession, a distinction becoming more and more blurred each year.

If law student recruits don't apprehend the true burden entailed in a 2,000 billable hour year, their lack of comprehension of the nature of a lawyer's life—especially a trial lawyer's—is even more critical.

Lawyers may be likened to verbal and psychological soldiers on the front lines of disputatious acrimony. They are just as in need of soulful R & R as any battle-weary grunt. That need goes beyond mere hours of work, just as a soldier's need to escape the battlefield has more to do with the character of the work than with the actual hours in battle. Indeed, some of the physical and emotional symptoms commonly reported by stressed-out lawyers are akin to those of post-traumatic stress syndrome in soldiers: the 3:00 a.m.

awakenings, the traumatic fixations, the depression, the emotional exhaustion, the resort to mind-altering chemicals.

The cumulative impacts upon a lawyer of higher billable hour budgets, more non-billable practice-related commitments, and the intrinsically stressful character of the practice of law combine to deaden or destroy ethereal human qualities, or soul. Lawyers whose careers span this transformation from manageable profession to overworked business treadmill express disenchantment bordering on sullen hostility, often without a clear understanding of the sources of their ennui.

Meanwhile, students who are racking up five-figure loans to pursue those big starting salaries have almost no meaningful concept of the life they will be expected to lead.

CHAPTER EIGHT

∾

# The APC Factor:
# The Truth about Clients

I wanted to become a lawyer to help people like Helen Palsgraf.

On August 24, 1924, Ms. Palsgraf went to the East New York station of the Long Island Railroad and bought a train ticket to Rockaway Beach. While she was standing on the platform awaiting her train, one bound for another destination arrived. Just as it began to depart, a last-minute passenger, a young man carrying a newspaper-wrapped package, ran down the platform and into the open door of the slowly moving train. He appeared to lose his balance momentarily, and two helpful guards of the Long Island Railroad, one aboard the train and another on the platform, reached to help him clamber aboard. As they did, the package was dislodged from his grip and fell on the rails.

Tragically for Helen Palsgraf but fortuitously for generations of American law students, the package contained fireworks, which "exploded with some violence" upon striking the rails. Many feet away down the platform, the concussion overturned some scales, which fell on the hapless Ms. Palsgraf, seriously injuring her. As she painfully convalesced, she sued the railroad for damages, and *Palsgraf v. Long Island Railroad Co.* became one of the best known cases in the history of American torts law.

Ms. Palsgraf won her case. The jury found the two railroad employees, and hence the railroad, committed the tort of negligence, and she was awarded damages. On appeal, however, her fortunes changed and a principle of torts law was created.

The question posed in the *Palsgraf* case was whether the New York appeals courts would permit Ms. Palsgraf to keep the money awarded based on the jury's finding of negligence. As virtually every law student who has studied the case can tell you, the plaintiff lost her case on appeal because Chief Justice Cardozo and the three New York judges who agreed with him decided that injury to the person harmed must be foreseeable from the tortious act. The court accepted the finding of negligence: the railroad guards, and hence the railroad, acted carelessly in helping a passenger board a moving train. But, given the somewhat convoluted chain of events that led to the injury to Ms. Palsgraf—the odd circumstance of the passenger's concealed explosive and the jarring loose of heavy objects many feet away to cause them to fall—the court concluded that the railroad was not liable. Some harm to someone was a possible result of the negligent acts, but the particular injury to Ms. Palsgraf was not reasonably foreseeable from those acts, so she lost her case.

The study of torts, that miscellaneous grab bag of claims for which courts have decided that a remedy in damages is warranted, begins to separate future lawyers from laity. Countless law students in their third week or so of law school have distanced themselves from friends or parents with some variant of: "I've got to go now. I need to parse a tort case before class tomorrow." They could just as accurately say they needed to summarize a personal injury court decision, but $25,000 a year in tuition, room and board is better justified by parsing torts.

The study of torts reinforces the mindset with which most of us enter law school. We assume normal people and companies running an honest business get enmeshed in disputes from time to time. Both sides need lawyers. This is the essence of our adversary system of resolving disputes. That one can make a starting salary of $65,000 a year and be a member of a respected profession are also powerful inducements, but the chance to help the lady next door who is injured by the toppling scales on the railroad platform was why I went to law school.

I soon realized, of course, that the Long Island Railroad needed a lawyer, too. While I visualized myself more readily as the plaintiff's champion, cases such as *Palsgraf* taught me that representing a corporation was also an honorable calling. Despite my sympathy for Ms. Palsgraf and my knowledge of the railroad's deep pockets, it was obvious that there must be limits to the railroad's liability for the behavior of some punk with a concealed bundle of cherry bombs who decides to ride their train. While the *Palsgraf* case dealt with a large corporate defendant, the law created by the court in that case seventy years ago could be applied to you or me the next time we drive a car or help a late-arriving passenger board a train. No, there was nothing wrong with being the railroad's lawyer. After all, he ultimately won the case.

The parties in the *Palsgraf* case, as is true with most of the non-criminal cases studied in American law schools, are innocent of any base behaviors or motives. By focusing on the study of such cases, the perception of law students is reinforced that clients are ordinary people embarked upon an honest search for justice.

In my experience, however, litigation clients, are seldom as pristine and pure as Helen Palsgraf appears in the pages of the appellate case reports. As a group, litigation clients are anything but ordinary, and, in fact, are wholly unrepresentative of the general populace. To be sure, sweet ladies like Ms. Palsgraf sometimes walk in the law firm door, but very few billable hours are racked up in pursuit of vindication for such totally faultless clients.

This truth of American lawyering can remain surprisingly elusive even to practicing attorneys. In the large law firms that increasingly dominate the private practice of law, it may be several years before a new trial lawyer realizes that clients' legal disputes are not merely the byproducts of society's routine mishaps and misunderstandings. But even making allowances for the obvious fact that most clients of bigger law firms are businesses or affluent individuals, the sampling of clients who walk through the trial lawyer's door even in America's elite law firms is anything but random.

Rare is the civil lawsuit that cannot be shaped by competent lawyers on both sides to look like a good faith disagreement between otherwise normal, decent, and honorable people. In most lawsuits there is some merit to each side's position. But this does not necessarily, or even usually, mean that the case is simply a dispute between ordinary folks.

Young trial lawyers in big law firms are almost always exceptionally credentialled and incisively bright, people who are the ultimate quick studies. Nevertheless, besides the inclination to assess a client only in relation to the opposition, two barriers work against their recognition of the true nature of typical litigation clients. First, to a greater extent than ever before, starting associates have little direct contact with clients. The crucial tone-setting consultations between the client and the law firm are conducted by the partner in charge of the file, and most knowledge of the client's character, motives, and objectives gained by the associates is filtered through that partner.

Second, no matter what the size of firm in which they practice, lawyers tend to minimize the faults of their clients. This reluctance to speak with candor is partly a matter of smart marketing—they may fear that the client will learn their true opinion of him or her or that other potential clients will be put off by a lawyer who speaks ill of any client. It is also partly due to ingrained behavior that becomes automatic after years of playing the role of advocate. We all want our clients to be wearing the white hat. Moreover, we are both taught and conditioned to balance all doubts in favor of the client. This combination of wishful thinking and instinctive advocacy leads invariably to a more rosy depiction of one's own clients than they deserve. Not only would our adversary contest this overly-favorable image we seek to paint, but even the client's close friends or relatives would sometimes acknowledge the client's flaws with greater readiness than his or her lawyer. We are, after all, paid advocates.

In fact, looking at America's litigation clients as a group, it might be more palatable for lawyers to contemplate the universe of their opponents' clients, rather than their own. I suspect most lawyers asked to expound upon the characteristics of adverse clients would agree. One's own clients might be okay, but other lawyers' clients are, as a group, indisputably more incompetent, more vindictive, less honest, more venal, and more greedy than the population as a whole.

What is true about the competition's clients is, of course, probably an accurate reflection of all clients everywhere, even after making allowances for the predisposition to disparage the other side. More often than we care to admit, people and companies entangled in major lawsuits are suing or being sued *because* their behavior deviates from the acceptable norm.

One of the significant sources of big litigation over the past decade has been the cases spawned by the turmoil following deregulation of the savings and loan industry in the 1980's. For fifty years or so, the people running savings banks were shielded from competition by federal law and highly restricted in the types of loans they were permitted to make. Most savings bank loans were small, given to finance the purchase of a home, a car, a boat. The bank officers who rose through the ranks to lead these S & L's acquired their experience with lending in this limited, hard-to-go-wrong context. Loan underwriting was largely a connect-the-dots procedure, assessing the security value of commonplace tangible property located in the vicinity of the S & L.

With deregulation in the early 1980's, these officers discovered almost overnight that their favored—admittedly anticompetitive—status *vis-à-vis* larger commercial banks had been eliminated. Suddenly, they were "free" to extend all types of loans anywhere in the country.

What happens when billions of dollars of other people's money passes through the hands of people inexperienced with big lending deals? What occurred was a colossal outpouring of manipulation, incompetence, and avarice, much of it at the hands of sharks outside the savings banks who quickly capitalized upon the rampant inexperience and gullibility they saw. Thrift officers in rural Ohio found themselves making multimillion-dollar construction loans for office buildings in suburban Houston, or financing a risky business venture in Los Angeles.

Following this loan underwriting free-for-all were lawsuits, thousands of them, brought to try to recover a fraction of the losses suffered through incompetence, mismanagement or fraud. And in every lawsuit, there were lawyers on each side, typically one representing the klutz and one representing the crook. As so often happens in such a matchup, especially in a society inclined to believe that a measure of sophistication attends the title of bank vice president, the dishonest side's conduct looked less opprobrious when weighed against the foolishness of the other side. A common defense was: "How could you have been so dumb as to make such a loan?"

In modern litigation, many of a lawyer's clients are more like a small-time Michael Milken than Helen Palsgraf. Or like a Rodney ("I don't get no respect") Dangerfield character, going through life muddling up their affairs and blithely blaming others. Law school visions die hard, but if the truth be faced squarely, in many cases neither side is pleasant to represent as a lawyer.

Follow the tentacles of most modern litigation back to the causative body of the dispute and you will find, more often than not, some type of aberrant behavior. Even if the case is between two large corporations, there is frequently a person or group of people whose contumacious conduct led to the lawsuit.

Every experienced trial lawyer can recall clients who deviate from society's norms by manifesting one or more of the following characteristics. Clients often are:

—Unyielding, unreasonable, and unable to see the other person's point of view.

—Fixated on the pursuit of money to the exclusion of other personal qualities or standards of decent conduct.

—Personally troubled, whether because they are in financial distress, suffering from alcoholism, dependent on other drugs, or mentally ill.

—Disputatious to the extent of thirsting for a fight.

—Downright dishonest.

—Incompetent and bumbling, often seeking to explain away their own shortcomings by blaming others.

—Moralistic or super-religious in their approach to life, leading to a form of self-righteous judgmentalism.

Law school teaches that justice is most likely to prevail if both miscreants and saints have good lawyers, and that it is not the moral burden of the lawyer to accept cases only from the deserving side. But the beginning associate in a premier law firm is usually led to believe that the clients of Pickering & Nosegay are cut from the finest bolt of virgin wool. By joining such a prestige firm, the associate has already opted out of a criminal defense practice, where many of a lawyer's clients are presumed to be deviants. The Pickering & Nosegay associate will never have to confront the question most commonly asked of aspiring lawyers: "Could you ever represent someone you *knew* was guilty?"

Because much of the riffraff has presumably been filtered out of the client rosters of major law firms, it is not difficult for young lawyers to accept the premise that the firm's clients are typically more deserving than their opponents, and certainly a blue ribbon sampling of society at large. When the associate first encounters a client whose moral standards incline more towards the felonious than fair-minded, it is difficult to put this encounter in perspective. Has he or she simply drawn the short straw from a hand full of mostly long straws? Is this one mean-spirited and vengeful client a rare aberration amidst the decent folks Pickering characteristically defends?

Occasionally, the partner in charge of a file drops a comment that offers a brief glimpse that contradicts the party line about the firm's clients. Tongue loosened by the third gin and tonic following settlement of the case, or when the client has failed to pay the bill, the partner may let slip a description of the client that flies in the face of all previous blandishments of virtue. The veil of adversarial discretion suddenly parts, and the illustrious Pickering & Nosegay's client suddenly is a "screw-up," a "jerk," or a "crook." In one summary epithet, the partner in charge reveals his or her reluctant conclusion after months or years of saying and wishing it weren't so.

As frequently as this happens, however, lawyers lack any framework for evaluating this isolated acknowledgment, this unguarded moment in which the client's behavior is described with utter accuracy. We are far more inclined to dismiss this client as an exception. Just because this one client proved to have lied about his case from the outset, or was revealed to be motivated more by vengeance than justice does not mean that our lot in life is to represent such people with regularity, we insist to ourselves. After all, most people are basically honest, and Pickering's clients are better than most.

It's not that good-guy clients never appear in a lawyer's life. It is refreshing to find a client who is reasonable, perceptive, and wronged, towards whom the earnestness of law school idealism kicks in with resounding fervor. Even a few such next-door-neighbor clients a year can boost a lawyer's morale.

But the self-deception practiced by many American lawyers is to generalize from these most deserving clients to the whole of their practice, a sure-fire guarantee of disillusionment in the long run.

To place the more typical experience of a trial lawyer in proper perspective, to describe with more accuracy the caseloads of those lawyers so as to understand the work they do and the life they lead, I have devised a pseudo-scientific method to measure the polyglot clients they represent. Some might call is it a contentiousness quotient, a rancor register, a malevolence meter. This standard could be used to compare the register of a firm's clients with other groups of people, such as the clients of other firms or the population at large. If lawyers can get beyond the rhetoric that their firm's clients are a large cut above the moral average and see them as they are, we may begin to reveal one of the root causes of disaffection with law practice.

In late-night conference rooms, at noisy bars, in living rooms with close colleagues, friends, and confidants, anywhere they kick off their shoes, loosen their ties, pull off their glasses and earrings, lawyers use one word more than any other to describe the type of clients who are all too present in any thriving practice these days. The likely subject of this epithet is the kind of client who can obsessively dominate one's waking thoughts and keep him or her up at night, invade a marriage for weeks on end, rule the lawyer's very existence, and generally cause trouble far out of proportion to the person's weight or worth. This word can be applied to the peevish incompetent client as well as to one who is darkly sinister. By informal consensus of usage, no single term, scatological or not, better describes those people ultimately responsible for the explosion of litigation in our country over the last thirty years, who cause endless headaches for lawyers and everyone else in their vicinity. This one word most employed by lawyers to vent their feelings about their worst clients is "asshole."

Using this lawyer's term of art for difficult clients, I suggest what I hope will be a helpful, if unscientific, formula for analyzing legal practice today: the APC Factor, measuring Assholes Per Capita.

Stated generally, the formula to determine the APC Factor in a given situation is:

$$\frac{\text{Assholes}}{\text{Total Population}} = \text{The APC Factor}$$

In the instance of American litigation clients, this formula would be more specifically stated as:

$$\frac{\text{Asshole Litigation Clients}}{\text{Total Litigation Clients}} = \begin{array}{c}\text{Litigation Client} \\ \text{APC Factor}\end{array}$$

For example, if we take the total number of new litigation clients in America last year (say 2,000,000) and determine the number of those litigants independently and objectively determined to be assholes (say approximately 800,000), the APC Factor is derived as follows:

$$\frac{800,000 \text{ Asshole Clients}}{2,000,000 \text{ Total Clients}} = .40 \text{ APC Factor}$$

While the actual research has not yet been done by law professors, sociologists, or whoever is best qualified to measure this phenomenon, my own experience and talks with other lawyers teach me that a typical APC Factor for litigation clients, even of elite law firms such as Pickering & Nosegay, is in the vicinity of .40 and rising. For comparative purposes, I would estimate that the APC Factor for all of American society, including those who are not parties to lawsuits, is closer to .10. If these rough empirical estimates are valid, the APC Factor for lawyers' clients is four times that of the overall populace, which leads us to:

LESSON EIGHT: *The APC Factor for a lawyer's clients is substantially higher than for the population at large.*

This lesson may appear to be self-evident. If so, and you're a third year law student, I suggest you ask the interviewer who comes to your law school from Pickering & Nosegay whether he or she acknowledges that the firm's litigation clients have a higher APC Factor than the overall average for his or her community, or even than the APC Factor for the congregants of the local Baptist church. You will, I predict, be met with a stream of soothing and confident assurances about the upstanding clients who choose to retain Pickering, coupled with a denial of any suggestion that these people could possibly be considered to be beneath the general moral mean of the community. They might add with a tone of muted candor that other law firms may, sadly, have clients whose motives are less pure and enlightened. But you can rest assured that P & N trial lawyers can be proud of their clients.

It may be true that Pickering & Nosegay's client APC Factor is the lowest of any law firm in town, even the lowest in the country. But be forewarned that even at the staid old Pickering firm you will be called upon to advocate for clients who will be, on average, far less sympathetic than Helen Palsgraf.

CHAPTER NINE

# *Market Day at the Legal Bazaar*

A t the time I finished law school in 1970, the "larger" law firms throughout the country were all expand-ing steadily in size, though the truly explosive growth was yet to come. The firm of 36 lawyers I then joined was the third largest in Minnesota. Today, less than 25 years later, while the population of the state has increased only slightly, a firm of 36 lawyers would be mid-sized at best. Nine firms have more than 100 lawyers, a number no state firm attained until the mid-1970's. It is the same in every area of the country. Most law firms have tripled or qua-drupled in size since 1970.

A fading photograph of the Hennepin County bench and bar that hangs in the local bar association offices highlights the change from an even earlier era. Taken in the late 1920's, the photograph shows the 200+ members of the bar asso-ciation at that time. There are now at least three *law firms*

125

larger than the entire bar was then, and the same county bar association has almost 7,000 members.

The majority of today's practicing lawyers entered the profession in these heady decades of double-digit growth. The firms prospered that "grew with their clients." Those that chose to remain smaller were, by and large, relegated to competitive backwaters, successful if they could maintain a specialty niche, like personal injury or real estate law, but hopelessly outgunned in any attempt to attract general business clients.

Two principal factors led to this exponential growth of major law firms throughout the country. First, their long-standing mainstay clients, the banks, businesses, and wealthy individuals they had represented for many years, demanded more and more legal services. Burgeoning government regulation at all levels led to a portion of this increase, and the rise in the incidence of litigation accounted for much of the rest. The meteoric rise in typical corporate budgets for legal expenses exactly paralleled the expansion of major law firms, much to the chagrin of the business world.

Second, in this growth era, the largest law firms were favored in comparison with their smaller competitors due to the economic benefits of legal specialization. Instead of having a lawyer who was proficient in the general practice of corporate law, for example, there emerged esoteric—and highly lucrative—specialists of all stripes: securities lawyers, merger and acquisition lawyers, and lawyers who matched their expertise to every form of governmental regulation, from OSHA to civil rights compliance. A firm that failed to evolve with the changes found itself losing clients to larger, more specialized firms that could summon an expert on short notice to deal, for example, with the fine points of new government regulations on credit disclosures or hazardous waste disposal. Gone were the days when a gifted generalist, the classic corporate legal counselor, could have a working understanding of all the major issues facing business clients. The law had become far too extensive and complex for any one person to serve as more than a coordinator of legal specialists.

Thus, there was both an absolute growth in individual clients' demands for legal help and a shifting of profitable specialized legal work from smaller to larger law firms, and these two factors combined to create a Golden Age for large law firms. Moreover, mere growth in the number of lawyers per firm does not tell the full story. The benefits of specialization also allowed large hikes in fees charged per hour of work. A corporation needing to know the most definitive interpretation of, say, subsection 21(g)(3) of a new FDA regulation would actually save money by paying a large firm's FDA specialist $300 per hour for advice rather than giving the same task to a less-specialized attorney whose hourly rate was only $100. More likely than not, the specialist could answer the question more authoritively in one hour of work than the generalist could in five.

An essential element of the rapid growth of large law firms, at least through about the mid '70's, was the stability of their existing client relationships, their client base. Each firm could be described by the clients whom, for the most part, they had served for many years. Banks and other business clients were distributed among law firms in a pattern that changed only slowly. Expansion of the larger firms, to the extent any lawyers lost out in this heyday, was at the expense of smaller ones, but First Bank and the XYZ Corporation tended to stay at the same firm as long as it grew to meet their needs. Families also kept the same "family lawyers" not only throughout one individual's life, but often through generations. One's lawyer was thought of as a trusted friend of the family.

Old traditions of the profession, enforced by strict prohibitions against lawyer advertising or solicitation of work, restrained everyone from "stealing" another's clients. Any attempt by another lawyer to solicit clients was deemed not only unethical, but also an interference with the proper workings of the professional relationship. Client solicitation was tantamount to slander; it was perceived as a criticism of the quality of one's legal advice, an act that could only undermine the sacrosanct attorney/client relationship. It just wasn't done.

The distribution of litigation legal work followed a similar pattern. Most businesses and many individuals had a long-term relationship with a law firm, and that firm's trial lawyers generally handled any litigation difficulties of "the firm's" clients.

As late as the mid '70's, in this milieu of stable long-term and unthreatened relations between lawyers and their clients, the need for legal services increased, but virtually no one "shopped" for a trial lawyer.

The overall heightened demand for legal services also benefited smaller law firms and sole practitioners in the '60's and '70's, though to a somewhat lesser extent and with more spotty impacts than was the case with the larger firms. Here also, the principle of loyalty to the family lawyer, or to the town lawyer, or to the small businessperson's lawyer, generally prevailed.

Prior to 1977, every state had strict rules against virtually any form of advertising by lawyers. Clients who felt uneasy with their existing counsel could not even look to the Yellow Pages for information about other attorneys. Lawyers could not even list such specialties as divorce, personal injury, or criminal law. So stringent was the advertising prohibition that bar associations regularly cautioned their members through published ethics opinions that almost any activity designed to draw attention to the lawyer was suspect. Some bar associations regulated the very size of the shingle that could be hung outside one's law office. My personal favorite at the time was the opinion forbidding lawyers from using blue stationery as law firm letterhead, for any paper hue other than shades of white or gray was deemed unprofessional.

Because most clients simply turned to the trial lawyer in the same firm handling their business or family matters for advice and representation, that lawyer had the leeway of placing the dispute in a long-term perspective. A wise lawyer of my acquaintance, who was in the prime of his practice during this era, summed up his experience in dealing with clients who, in the heat of disputatious passion, wanted to bring a lawsuit that shouldn't have been brought. "I never lost a client by counseling against litigation," he said. Against the backdrop of a longstanding relationship of trust, his clients were willing to heed advice that ran against the strongly felt ardor of the moment.

All this has changed. In 1977 the United States Supreme Court struck down most restrictions on lawyer advertising as unconstitutional infringements of the right of commercial free speech. Almost overnight, radio, television, and newspaper ads appeared. Where once it was improper to list one's name in the telephone directory in bold-face type, lawyer ads, many occupying a splashy full page, now consume more of the Yellow Pages than any other business or profession. Lawyers' names appear on everything from baseball park placards to ball point pens to bowling shirts.

But the advent of lawyer advertising is only one event in a far broader transformation of the law market. As far as attracting clients is concerned, the evolution of the practice of law from a profession to a business is virtually complete. Lawyers vie with each other for clients, even business clients, with unprecedented vigor. The most staid and biggest firms aggressively woo clients from their competitors, even as their own clients are being solicited. One-on-one client solicitation that was thought to be unspeakably unethical in 1970 is now routine.

To some extent, unwitting though it may have been, the larger firms presaged this more commercial approach to law through their own expansion. As long as growth was exclusively at the expense of smaller, less specialized, firms, they could smugly attribute any realignment of clients into the hands of big firms to the inexorable superiority of their economies of scale.

Growth takes on a momentum of its own, however, and sooner or later they were bound to turn their voracious appetites for expansion into direct competition with firms their own size. The lifting of the advertising ban simply came at an opportune time. Though bigger firms still eschew the most blatant forms of consumer-directed advertising, they all engage in "marketing" of their services with a vengeance.

Now that the stringent rules and traditions of yesteryear are history, individuals and companies routinely shop for a trial lawyer. Theoretically, these changes should liberate clients to pick the most reasonably priced, competent, and experienced lawyer to handle their problem. What is happening in the marketplace, however, is shaded a little darker. When the Assistant Vice President of the XYZ Corporation's overbearing and irascible management style has led to the prospect of rancorous litigation with disgruntled former employees, gone are the days when he or she automatically seeks legal aid from the litigation department of good old Pickering & Nosegay.

Now, a search is conducted, often with the goal of finding a lawyer who is deemed sufficiently aggressive to stand up to or wear down the lawyer who represents those sniveling malcontents who have dared to sue the company. Quite often, the executive in charge of the search is the very person most inflamed by the dispute, and the person responsible for creating the crisis in the first place. Unfettered by the tradition of consulting a permanent legal counselor, the client whose conduct would elevate the APC Factor of any company goes with increasing frequency in search of a like-minded lawyer.

Who will be hired as the result of such a search? You can rest assured, or be forewarned, that it will not be the lawyer who counsels prudence, deliberation, or caution. It will more likely be the one who most convincingly shows that he or she will obtain the money, the vindication, or the vengeance sought, or who best panders to the potential client's idiosyncratic goals. Such clients most often get just what they want—and more: a hyper-aggressive lawyer who charges enormous fees to whip up the lawsuit to a fever pitch that precludes any conciliatory or inexpensive solution.

Consider the canine similes used so often these days by clients in their search for a trial lawyer. What we need to handle the SOB on the other side of this case, they say, is a bulldog, a Doberman, a pit bull, an attack dog. The ideal lawyer, it seems, is just a snarl short of rabid. Granted, nobody wants a cocker spaniel for a lawyer. But the stolid St. Bernard, calm, assured, and ready to assist, is endangered, too. More and more, the lawyer marketing rewards go to those with the longest fangs.

Now that the tradition of professional loyalty and stability has given way to the turmoil of the marketplace, we need to understand the forces of supply and demand that are shaping the practice of law. The aggregation of individual decisions made by clients when hiring trial lawyers makes up the demand side of the marketplace equation. Those demands mold the supply side, the trial lawyers who are available to furnish the needed legal services. In a market in which clients shop for lawyers, the traits and behaviors sought by those clients will be reinforced under the immutable economic rules set forth by Adam Smith.

Once again, use of the APC Factor might help us to analyze the dynamic forces at work in this relatively novel shifting of legal work among trial lawyers. According to classical theories of economics, market demand is created by overall trends, and economic actors modify their behavior to maximize their perception of the present and future expected course of those trends. People with a direct stake in the legal profession, be they pre-law or law students or law-yers, has a vital interest in the question: What is the nature of the demand for trial lawyers in the legal marketplace, and how does it stack up against the currently available sup-ply?

Once again, until detailed social science studies are avail-able, I rely upon empirical evidence and discussions with many trial lawyers. On that basis, I offer:

LESSON NINE: *The APC Factor for clients is currently higher than for lawyers, even if one limits the field to trial lawyers.*

Many readers, including some lawyers, will fight the con-clusion that *any* group of people has a higher APC Factor than trial lawyers. But considering the context of this par-ticular market, I believe any objective study would confirm this observation.

It may indeed be arguable that bankers, plumbers, or in-surance salespersons would each, taken as a group, have a lower APC Factor than trial lawyers. Our inquiry, however, is limited to those who sue or get sued, thus becoming cli-ents. In economic terms, the demand of plumbers for trial lawyer services is created not by the pool of all plumbers, but by the subgroup of plumbers who get enmeshed in le-gal problems or litigation. As observed in the last chapter, people involved in lawsuits—be they plumbers, bankers, or neighbors—are as a group more different from their fellow citizens than they are like them.

Lawyers are not exposed to every facet of their clients' behavior or lives, but only to that part that leads them into legal difficulties. Most religious evangelists, for example, spend their lives doing good works and helping people. They seldom need the services of a trial lawyer. Should an evangelist be accused of pilfering church funds, however, or of sexually harassing Sunday School teachers or students, the trial lawyer who represents him or her may encounter a client who is more difficult and more sanctimoniously hostile to his or her accusers than the most dishonest corporate manipulator or even the average street criminal.

Lawyers often see clients in their worst light, and clients commonly make their decisions to hire lawyers at a time when their behavior is uncharacteristically abominable. It matters nothing to the legal marketplace equation that the behavior of evangelists is pure most of the time, if they act like scoundrels when they are retaining a trial lawyer. The APC Factor for evangelists may be only .02, but it is the .50 Factor for those retaining trial lawyers that sets the climate for the legal profession.

Every lawyer's practice is filled with normally good people whose foibles and frailties are highlighted by the disputes that led them into litigation. Now, once such clients embark upon the demand side of the trial lawyer shopping spree, they are as likely to look for the same rabidly aggressive lawyer as more recognizable miscreants.

Another factor to weigh in the modern legal marketplace is the unequal demand *among* clients for legal services. Stated succinctly, and I think irrefutably, the clients with the highest APC Factors are likely to soak up the most legal work—and to generate the largest number of billable hours. When reasonable people get in disagreements, be they evangelists, bankers, or plumbers, they are more likely to find a means of solving the problem short of a pitched legal battle. They may require the help of a lawyer in doing so—a well-worded letter often suffices—but they seldom generate big bucks in legal fees. A former partner of mine once described the ideal client as a "wholly unreasonable rich man." His unreasonableness creates the demand for lawyers, and he must be rich to pay their fees.

To date, the APC Factor still remains higher for clients than for lawyers. Unlike the futures market for pork bellies, the legal marketplace functions slowly and imperfectly. Many lawyers openly fight the transformation from profession to commerce. Others are too old to change their ways and continue to counsel their (dwindling) client caseload by urging decency and restraint. Both law firms and law schools continue to foster the myth that clients are merely representative of society, thereby implicitly conveying the impression that a market exists for the civilized lawyer who provides straight advice at a reasonable fee. The truth is closer to the opposite:

> FIRST COROLLARY TO LESSON NINE: *In America today, there is a surfeit of decent lawyers and a deficit of asshole lawyers.*

Not enough asshole lawyers? Society may erupt in disputing such an outrageous contention. Bear in mind, however, that we are discussing economic principles. If the supply of the kind of lawyers available still falls short of the demand, the APC Factor for trial lawyers will be driven higher and higher until it closely approximates that of clients. Supply seeks equilibrium with demand.

Two final observations flow logically from this discussion:

COROLLARY TWO TO LESSON NINE: *The law firms with the highest APC Factors are most likely to succeed financially in today's market.*

COROLLARY THREE TO LESSON NINE: *The student "most likely to succeed" in any law school class is the brightest asshole.*

Perhaps I overstate the point. Perhaps it is not too late to step back from the course charted over the last 25 years toward a lower and nastier common denominator. Perhaps clients themselves can be made to see the folly in solving every problem with a lawsuit, in waging every lawsuit like the siege of Leningrad. Perhaps the legislatures, the lawyers, or the courts can find ways to discourage those who would be legal pit bulls, be they client or lawyer. Perhaps.

In the meantime, unless something changes, given the immutability of economic laws, sooner or later clients will get exactly the sort of lawyers they demand—and deserve.

# EPILOGUE

As I was writing this book, I showed drafts to some of my closest friends who are lawyers. After reading it, they poured out thoughts about their own lives and related anecdotes from their law practices. During these conversations, it became evident to me that the lessons which I had learned, often painfully, were striking deeply buried but highly sensitive nerves within them, and I was struck with the quiet passion with which their reactions were expressed.

A couple of friends feared that the book might dwell too much on the negative aspects of being a lawyer without showing enough of the good parts. To this comment, I offered an unabashed plea of guilty with specific intent. I chose to write about the soft unexposed underbelly of lawyering, but not because I dislike lawyers or wish to paint a pejorative picture of their lives—far from it.

Rather, I found myself thinking most about those lawyers who have risen to the peak of our profession, have experienced all the "good parts," and are disenchanted nonetheless. I found myself dwelling on the tens of thousands of students who flood the law schools with their applications, largely oblivious to the lives they will lead as lawyers. Even in this age of lawyer-bashing, the overwhelming preponderance of society's messages about law and lawyering still portray a falsely rosy image of the lives of lawyers, and more laws and lawsuits are still touted as the answers to every human problem. Both lawyers and students stand to benefit from seeing the rigors, emotional burdens, and realities of lawyering with greater clarity.

I am prepared to accept responsibility that a few pre-law students well-suited to be lawyers will elect another career, distressed that a lawyer's life offers nothing better than I have described. That America will be damaged by some of its best students electing not to become lawyers is the least of my fears. The pendulum has swung so far towards favoring legalistic solutions that even if I offered an unfairly negative picture—and I do not believe I have—it would likely have a salutary effect of moving that pendulum closer to the center. If a handful of pre-law students reflect on the lessons of this book and decide to become engineers, ministers, priests, rabbis, teachers, carpenters, or business leaders instead of lawyers, most of them will be the better for it, and the country will not suffer. There is absolutely no chance that America will face a lawyer shortage in the foreseeable future.

I could fill pages with stories of the many ways I have seen lawyers help people, just as any soldier could tell tales of the kind and constructive acts of the troops. I chose, instead, to describe the parts of lawyers' lives invariably glossed over or relegated to footnotes in the paeans to our profession. In so doing, it was and is my hope to help explain the discrepancy between image and reality, between lawyers' publicly expressed satisfaction with their jobs and privately manifested depression and desperation with their careers as lawyers, between a profession that exalts itself as a helping force while compelling its members to hurt people.

A few of those who read my early draft manuscript felt frustrated that the book fails to prescribe remedies for the ills it discusses. But the first step towards addressing any set of problems is a detailed descriptive diagnosis, and I found myself unwilling—unable, even—to leap to issuing prescriptions until that diagnosis was clear. We can-do, optimistic Americans are prone to rush to provide answers before the questions are accurately framed.

Some day we may look back on the orgy of lawyering that marked our country's history from 1960 to 2000 with the same mixture of wonderment and scorn now reserved for such misadventures as Prohibition and Vietnam. From that future perspective, we will blame lawyers no more than we blame the WCTU or Carrie Nation for Prohibition or Lyndon Johnson for Vietnam. When we examine our history honestly, we will blame ourselves for the excesses of our own shortcomings of observation, our profound naiveté, our fixation with solving problems leading to the creation of other problems bigger than those we sought to correct.

I suspect we Americans at some future time will be struck by the colossal wrong-headedness of the notion that if due process is a good concept, then three times the process is three times as good. We will shake our heads over the very idea that the best solution to every complex human quandary is more laws, more legal remedies, and more lawyers.

Future historians will unearth the files of an actual case that was brought in my community several years ago. A dog owner sued a microwave oven manufacturer for failing to post a warning label alerting her to the fact she could not dry out her shampooed pet poodle with a three-minute zap, as she had always done before in her convection oven. They will marvel at the price we all paid for creating a system of legal remedies that provided no effective deterrents to such nonsense. They will express incredulity at our willingness to throw legal fixes at problems far better solved through compromise; through moral, ethical, or spiritual leadership; or through less antagonistic and costly methods than litigation.

But all that lies in the future. For now, I am content to describe rather than prescribe, to provoke debate rather than calm troubled waters, simply to offer readers my personal observations about lawyers and the climate in which they work.

The thoughts I express here are merely an outline of one lawyer's perspective. How much richer this story could be if told from the vantage points of the many people who care enough about lawyers to read this book, who care enough about our legal system to question where it is going.

## About the Author

Walt Bachman has been an attorney since 1970. In his unusually varied legal career, he has been a litigating partner in both small and large law firms, a chief deputy district attorney, and, for three years, the chief prosecutor in state legal ethics cases. He has law degrees from Oxford University, where he was a Rhodes Scholar, and from Stanford University. A past bar association president, he served on the ABA's Standing Committee on Ethics and Professional Responsibility and has taught and lectured widely on legal ethics issues. He lives in Minneapolis, Minnesota.